SoulSifting

SoulSifting

Exploring Our Spiritual Needs

R. Scott Sullender

WIPF & STOCK · Eugene, Oregon

SOULSIFTING
Exploring Our Spiritual Needs

Wipf & Stock
An Imprint of Wipf and Stock Publishers
199 W. 8th Ave., Suite 3
Eugene, OR 97401

www.wipfandstock.com

PAPERBACK ISBN: 979-8-3852-6691-3
HARDCOVER ISBN: 979-8-3852-6692-0
EBOOK ISBN: 979-8-3852-6693-7

VERSION NUMBER 04/23/26

Contents

Acknowledgments

THE ORIGINS OF THIS book lie in my forty-five years of clinical practice, but its blossoming in more recent years is due in large measure to the support, insights, and creativity of the Tuesday Morning Group at the Interfaith Counseling Center, San Anselmo, California. I appreciate and am grateful for the miracle of community.

This book is dedicated to all of the "seekers" out there, those of you who seek a more authentic experience of God, often along nontraditional pathways. This book is dedicated to you. Keep on seeking—what you seek is closer than you can imagine.

Introduction

We human beings have many needs. We have physical needs for food, water, oxygen, and sleep. We have health needs—to be free from physical pain, to grow. We have psychological needs for safety, for self-esteem, for motivation, and for love. We have intellectual needs for mental stimulation, to understand life and the world around us. We have social needs for belonging and community. Suppose, just suppose, we also have spiritual needs.

Need theory implies that we are not fully functioning or fully healthy without our needs being fulfilled to some degree. Indeed, we know that we cannot be physically healthy unless we have adequate food, water, and sleep. Without fulfilling these needs, we become sick. Our health declines. Such deficits can even hasten our death.

Similarly, we cannot be emotionally or mentally well unless our psychological needs satisfied. If we live with chronic low self-esteem, without love, or in situations where our safety is constantly an issue, we will decline as surely as we would with inadequate sleep or food. Signs of unmet psychological needs can include depression, anxiety, aggression, and nightmares. This dynamic is especially obvious when it comes to children. Children who grow up without love or security and/or in situations where they are verbally abused often do not mature into healthy adults. We know this, right?

Now consider the realm of the spirit. Suppose we humans, as I am proposing, have certain basic spiritual needs. If so, then getting those spiritual needs satisfied, at least most of the time, would be necessary for spiritual health. If the need for meaning, for example, is fulfilled, then we will live our lives with purpose and direction. If we fail to have our need for meaning satisfied, we may drift through life without purpose and direction. How about the need for hope? If our need for hope is fulfilled, then we will endure times of suffering with patience and resilience. If we do not have hope, we may despair in times of trial. We may become discouraged. We may become cynical. In such circumstances, we might say we are spiritually ill or spiritually deficient, and this might contribute to a decline in our psychological, mental, social, and even physical health. Our spiritual health is an important ingredient in our overall well-being.

How Important Are Our Spiritual Needs?

Some of the more basic human needs, like for food, rest, and water, are survival needs. If these survival needs are not satisfied, they scream for our attention. Similarly, our psychological and social needs can clearly and persistently demand our attention. However, if we lack hope, purpose, forgiveness, a moral code, or inner peace, these needs have more subtle ways of getting our attention. They are just as likely to nudge at our soul as they are to shout at us. This is so because most of our spiritual needs overlap with our psychosocial needs and/or are partially fulfilled by ordinary social and psychological processes. Thus, we do not recognize them as a pressing need. Our spiritual needs are partially or artificially satisfied in ways that take the edge off our hunger. We limp along in life until a crisis arises.

The various human needs have sometimes been presented graphically in the form of a pyramid, ascending from the physical to the higher needs, sometimes called our growth needs or our self-actualizing needs. Spiritual needs are to be understood as a part of these "higher needs." Our physical needs are in the large base at the bottom of the pyramid. If our physical needs for food or water are not met, so the argument goes, all other activities stop until those needs are addressed. Our physical needs are foundational. We cannot be concerned about art or about self-worth, and certainly not about the meaning of life, if we are starving or thirsty. As our more basic needs are met, we can increasingly refocus our energies on securing our psychological and social needs, and as these needs are met, we can pay attention to our higher needs for beauty, meaning, growth, etc. This model is commonly called the hierarchy of needs.

In everyday life, this hierarchical classification of needs is not always so neat and tidy. Most of us flow in and out of various categories of need throughout the day and throughout the various stages of our lives. Few of us have all of our needs met all of the time. Most of us live with varying degrees of need fulfillment. Getting our needs met is not an either/or proposition. Furthermore, it is not easy to classify many human activities as being driven by one need alone. Some human activities actually address needs found in several levels of the pyramid. For example, sexual relationships address our physical need for sexual release, our psychological need for closeness and love, and even our social need to create a family.

Spiritual needs are usually placed at the top of this classic pyramid model, and they certainly depend on the more foundational needs being addressed first and foremost. But what if spiritual needs also run as threads throughout the entire pyramid? Sometimes, people at the base of the pyramid with the most pressing physical needs, such as prisoners of war or those with a chronic disability, are more focused on their spiritual needs and the fulfillment of those spiritual needs than we might imagine. Their intense physical needs give the fulfillment of their spiritual needs greater urgency and may help them endure their state of physical deficiency.

In other words, all of our needs are interrelated and interconnected. Being physically ill can impact our spiritual need for hope and courage, just as our lack of hope and courage can contribute to our physical illness. Human health and well-being includes all of our needs—physical, social, psychological and spiritual.

How to Know If You Are Spiritually Hungry or Malnourished

The absence of food and water will make us sick, but so will junk food and impure water. If we regularly eat food that is of poor nutritional quality, our health will suffer. Similarly, in the world of our psyches, how we get our psychological needs met matters as much as the fact that we get them met at all. For instance, consider our need for love. Some of us will get their need for love met by their family. Others will get their need for love met by a dog. And still others will seek out the services of a prostitute. Some people stay in abusive relationships for years and years. Why? Their need for love is so intense, they will put up with great humiliation and the risk of life and limb.

Or consider our need to belong—to be a part of a community of peers who know us and accept us. We humans are very social, relational creatures, aren't we? This social need is particularly acute during our adolescent years. Some teenagers fulfill this need by participating in a youth group at church, others by belonging to a clique or club at school, and still others by joining a local street gang. Clearly, *how* the need is met is as important as *whether* the need is met at all, and in the case of our spiritual needs the *how* is even more important!

The strength of a person's spiritual needs will vary from person to person and from need to need. Not all of us will experience the same urgency or will manifest our spiritual hunger the same way. In this book, we will explore some of our basic spiritual needs and in each case will touch on signs of their absence and malnourishment. *How* we get our spiritual needs met matters. There are life-enriching and life-robbing ways of addressing our spiritual needs.

What Do We Mean by Spiritual? Is It the Same as Religious?

"Spirituality" is a vague, ambiguous, and at times paradoxical term. It is widely employed to cover a multitude of experiences. In this book, I begin by drawing on the original meaning of the word "psyche," which is the soul, mind, or spirit of a person. Spirituality refers to a reality beyond what we can see, touch, hold, and manipulate, a reality that is beyond space and time. It refers to dynamics beyond ourselves and yet, at the same time, at the core of our being. Spirituality is our connection to or relationship with this nonmaterial reality. Spirituality includes the traditional concept of God (with all that "God" might mean), angels, and our ancestors. It also encompasses our values, ideals, ultimate meanings, intuitions, mystical experiences, and life philosophy. Obviously, then, the content or "stuff" of spirituality can vary widely from person to person. The focus in this book is not on whether your spirituality is right or wrong but on whether it satisfies your deepest spiritual needs in ways that enable you to thrive. That is the critical question that runs as a theme throughout this book.

The center of spirituality in each of us is traditionally called our soul, our spirit, our divine spark, or our consciousness. Our soul or psyche is both unique to each of us and also universal; all of us have a capacity for or hunger for spirituality. Amid the pressing demands of daily life, we tend to ignore our spiritual self in favor of our material self. The latter seems more real and, like I said, more pressing. Or, we manage by throwing our soul tidbits, leftovers, or even toxic material in the hope that doing so will quiet the starving soul within.

Sometimes, spirituality is used as a synonym for the mystical, irrational, or unexplainable. This is an unfortunate dichotomy. The desire to understand, to gain knowledge, and to satisfy our longing to figure out reality is part of the spiritual quest and, in my view, is a spiritual need. Sometimes, spirituality is used as a synonym for a person's inner life. This too is an unfortunate dichotomy because true spirituality has a transpersonal dimension, a way of connecting us to others. Nevertheless, coming up with a clear definition of spirituality continues to be challenging. Avoiding some of this vagueness is the reason I prefer the concept of spiritual needs.

Religion gives institutional expression to human spirituality. Religion, in its various forms and expressions, exists to address humanity's deep spiritual needs. Each religion offers its adherents pathways to regularly fulfill those needs. All that we think of as religion—doctrines, rituals, congregations, and clergy—exist to fulfill our spiritual needs, although many will argue that organized religion can lose and has lost its way, sometimes existing more for its own institutional needs than for the fulfillment of the needs of its members. It should be noted, of course, that there are many religions out there, as well as many denominations within the major faith traditions and many quasi-religious entities, cults (religious and political), and movements or "isms." All of these "religions" fulfill in part or in full various spiritual needs we have. Organized religion is certainly the most common avenue through which most people get their spiritual needs met, but as you read this book, I hope it will be obvious that people can fulfill or try to fulfill their spiritual needs in ways outside of organized religion.

Furthermore, it should also be obvious that particular religions, denominations, and faith communities vary widely in their ability to meet humanity's spiritual needs. Some religious traditions or denominations emphasize one or two of our spiritual needs while giving only passing or indirect attention to other needs. These variations are due to cultural and historical factors. While spiritual needs are universal, their expressions—the paths available to fulfill them and the language and symbols employed to express those needs—vary from culture to culture and population to population.

As an example, many would suggest that we humans have a need to devote ourselves to something or someone greater than ourselves, sometimes with passionate dedication. By so doing, we infuse our otherwise ordinary lives with meaning, purpose, significance, and community. For many people around the globe, this need is fulfilled through devotion to a religion or religious deity. In more modern secular societies, where addiction in its varied forms is becoming a mental health epidemic, it is possible that our spiritual need for devotion has been highjacked by the addiction process. In other words, addiction is at its root a misplaced longing for God, turning the object of our addiction into our god and thus fulfilling our need for devotion.

The same dynamic can be seen in people who are overly devoted to their nation, to a political leader, to a social-political cause, to a professional sports team, to their business or career, to an institution, to an activity, or, even more commonly, to their children and family. Like religion, these nonreligious or spiritual devotions can have life-giving or toxic and destructive side effects. How well do you think these alternative passions or objects of our devotion fulfill our spiritual need to give ourselves to something greater than ourselves?

Do We All Have the Same Spiritual Needs?

Yes and no. It does seem like there are universal, basic spiritual needs. I will discuss in subsequent chapters what I think are our twenty-two universal spiritual needs. Yet, people experience the strength of each spiritual need differently, and a given spiritual need will manifest itself differently in each individual, depending on their temperament, culture, and life experience. Some of us will find certain spiritual needs or clusters of several spiritual needs exciting, energizing, and engaging, whereas others will find these same needs uninteresting. I would say that there are different pathways to God. Each spiritual need represents a different pathway to connect with the Divine. Spirituality is wonderfully diverse and inclusive in that regard. Some meet God in the silence of a retreat and some in the view through a telescope, in helping the needy, in the majesty of a symphony, or in taking courageous steps. And, of course, some meet God in a large religious gathering. There are multiple pathways to the realm of the Spirit.

In the chapters that follow, I describe twenty-two basic spiritual needs, concluding with the need for beauty, which is both a need and a tool by which we may explore all of our spiritual needs. Admittedly, the terms and words I use to describe each need may appear ambiguous. Some of these needs overlap, making them less distinctive or clear. Our words sometimes fail us when it comes to describing things we cannot see. Perhaps the language of the poets, artists, or mystics is more suitable to an exploration of our spiritual needs. We do not have a clear and universally understood spiritual language. Words and terms mean different things to different people. In the chapters that follow, I do my best to describe each need as clearly as possible as well as what happens when a particular need is or is not fully satisfied.

Our spiritual needs are rooted in the "givens" of human existence and as such cannot be satisfied or resolved fully in ordinary human ways. The resolution or fulfillment of these needs lies in the realm of the Spirit, in concepts, principles, or perspectives that are beyond flesh-and-blood experiences in life. A spiritual need is, by definition, a need that (1) is rooted in a given of human existence, or what has been called the "human condition," and (2) cannot be fulfilled or satisfied without reaching for something beyond ourselves, beyond space and time, beyond the rational, materialistic, and scientific realms to the realm of the Divine.

How Do We Distinguish Our Spiritual Needs from Our Other Needs?

In spite of the above definition of spiritual needs, we can also see clearly that many spiritual needs are partially met by psychological, social, and even physical processes. The issue is further complicated by the fact that most faith communities seek to meet a variety of their members' needs, not just their spiritual needs. Congregational life can fulfill some psychological needs—helping people process their grief, helping them feel good about themselves, and building confidence. Faith groups can also fulfill social needs—for community, for belonging, for support in times of hardship, and for safety. Some religious communities also fulfill the economic and physical needs of their members—for food, shelter, medical treatment, and business contacts. So, yes, each spiritual need can be partially satisfied through ordinary, human processes and institutions in and outside of the world of religion.

Another example is our need for forgiveness, which can be and often is fulfilled through such human processes as the criminal justice system, conflict mediation, or family therapy. Yet, I suggest that forgiveness also has an element that is spiritual in nature. While our need for forgiveness can be largely fulfilled through human processes, there is a kind of forgiveness or unique occasions requiring forgiveness that can only be addressed through spiritual channels, through a reaching beyond the human plane. I clarify the uniquely spiritual nature of the spiritual need discussed in each chapter that follows.

Religion in a Consumer Marketplace

Modern America is a consumer-oriented culture. People seeking a religion or God often approach a new congregation, unconsciously or consciously, with the question, "Does this church or faith community fill my or my family's needs?" The question that they should be asking, however, is, "Does this religion or congregation fill my spiritual needs?" I'm afraid that, more often than not, most people, religious or otherwise, select a new church not so much based on a careful self-assessment of their spiritual needs but on the marketplace appeal of the congregation's social programs, economic opportunities, attention to their family's needs, and location and market appeal. To be good consumers of religion, however, we need to do better than this! Yes, religion can address our psychological, social, and economic needs, but not at the expense of a vibrant spiritual life or, more precisely, without integrating the rest of our life with a vibrant spiritual life that addresses our spiritual needs in life-affirming ways. So, first we need to understand what our spiritual needs are, how to recognize our needs, and the signs of a lack of fulfillment of those needs. We need to be able to differentiate between healthy and toxic need fulfillment and between our true spiritual needs and our psychological and social needs. In short, we need to learn to "read the labels" so we can find healthy and balanced ways to fulfill our spiritual needs.

In traditional cultures and earlier centuries of Western culture, the spiritual needs of people were provided for in more structured ways by institutions and culture. People held a more uniform worldview; everyone knew their place, and their purpose was defined by their role and status. Spirituality was expressed in ritual. Meaning was offered and mediated by religious leaders. In modern and postmodern culture, however, fewer vital institutions provide for our spiritual needs. Everything is up for grabs, and we live in a world with more fragmentation, more relativism, and less consensus on values and truth. In Western consumer cultures, few of us have our religion handed to us anymore. We must learn to be proactive in finding and sustaining our spiritual needs, just as we do our physical, economic, and social needs. Furthermore, today we do not need to stay with whatever religion we were born into (if any). We can choose. We can shop around. We can compare. We can investigate. We can and must seek—if we wish to find.

The challenge today is that most of the traditional and institutional ways that we once got our spiritual needs met have faded. In their place, we have a whole host of "products" that are spiritually poisonous. We are vulnerable to the cunning deceit of people and institutions that use our spiritual needs against us, leaving us with toxicity instead of life. In religion as well as economics, the motto is now "Buyer beware." We need to become wise consumers in relation to our spiritual needs, just as we must be wise consumers in relation to our physical needs, medical needs, psychological needs, and social needs.

I hope that this book will appeal to and be used by readers who are not religious ("nones") and people who are religious but seeking a deeper spiritual walk ("seekers"). Religious professionals who care for such people may also find this book helpful. In all cases, I hope readers will treat this book like a workbook. Reflect on each chapter and use the reflection questions and activities at the end of each chapter to guide you in exploring the particular spiritual need it addresses. Finally, I hope that this book will help you *sift* through your *soul* by discerning your spiritual needs—identifying them, affirming them, and fulfilling them in healthy ways.

Most of all, I hope that you enjoy the journey.

Scott Sullender
Petaluma, California
www.scottsullender.com

1

Meaning

Making Meaning of Life's Random Nature

LIFE IS RANDOM. THE raw experience of life happens randomly, seemingly without meaning, purpose, or predictable patterns. This is the nature of human existence, an aspect of the way things are in this universe. Out of this condition arises one of our most basic spiritual needs: the need for meaning.

In the English language, the word "meaning" and its derivatives have several nuanced uses, as illustrated in the following phrases: "What is the meaning of these events?" (explanation), "You are meaningful to me!" (significance), "It was meant to be" (purpose). In subsequent chapters, we will explore these spiritual needs embedded in meaning. In this chapter, I focus on the use of the word as it relates to the meaning of life, particularly the random nature of life.

Primitive humans constantly scanned the environment looking for patterns. They searched for similar colors and for familiar events that might signal a seasonal change, the location of food, or the presence of danger. Finding patterns in the environment was essential to their survival. We humans have become quite good at identifying patterns in otherwise random stimuli—making meaning out of random data points.

- We modern humans are still looking for patterns—but not so much in nature as in our lived experience.
- When events seemingly repeat themselves, we suspect a pattern.

- When we experience coincidences that cannot be explained, we suspect a hidden purpose.
- When the odds are dramatically for us or against us, we believe our good fortune or bad luck to be the result of something we did.
- When tragedies happen without fairness, we suspect a larger plan, even a secret conspiracy.
- When we are confused by the present moment, we draw on dreams, visions, memories, or even prophecies to provide meaning.
- When we find a pattern, we affirm that what happened was "meant to be" or that it was "part of God's plan."

Humans are meaning-*seeking* creatures. If meaning is not readily apparent, we are meaning-*making* creatures. The experience of meaninglessness is quite horrifying. Only the strongest among us can look it straight in the eye. Most of us are quick to make meanings, however partial, temporary, or even toxic they may be. Sometimes, identifying an irrational meaning feels better than seeing no meaning at all.

One of the more common ways we make meaning is through storytelling. Through stories, we transform the raw experience of life into a meaningful pattern. Stories say both "Here is what happened" and "Here is what it means." Stories can take the form of literature, drama, songs, poems, and history. Some stories are so transgenerational and universal that they become vehicles of spiritual truths more than narratives of historical facts. Scholars call such stories "myths." Myths, like all stories, are the carriers of meaning; myths carry cultural meaning.

The need for meaning can reach a crisis point in our lives when we face loss, suffering, or unwelcome change. When we stand at the grave of a loved one, watch an innocent child suffer, or are coping with an unexpected challenge, our meaning system is tested. If it is weak or nonexistent, our need for meaning itself becomes part of the crisis. We experience an existential "crisis of meaning." But what is true in crisis mode is also true in the rest of life. We need meaning every day of our lives. We need meaning

to survive,
  to thrive, and
    to enjoy life.

A woman I will call Denise was caught in traffic trying to rush to the airport to make an important business flight to the West coast. Every shortcut she tried proved futile. Every stoplight she came to was red. She even was delayed by a train—one of those slow-moving freight trains that took forever to pass. Well, she missed her flight, of course, and fumed and fussed and then went down the black hole of negativity. The next day, she learned that her missed flight had had engine trouble and was diverted to another airport to make an emergency landing. She paused, took a deep breath, and sighed. "I was supposed to be on that flight! I would not have made it to my meeting even if I had made that flight." Was this seemingly random event a sign or a message—or was it just coincidence?

Weeks later, Denise had a "revelation." She felt that God had intervened on that day, blocking her from attending the meeting. She was excited and felt lucky. She was not sure why God had intervened, but for the moment, she was happy. She had meaning. She had a story. And it made sense. Now open to what God might be trying to tell her, she reviewed her career direction and priorities. In time, she came to change careers and made other changes in her lifestyle that were all pretty positive and further reinforced her story that her career in business was not "meant to be." "God had a different plan for my life," she said, and the missed flight was "the first step." This is the meaning she made out of the random event of missing her plane.

Denise had a religious "map" or cognitive framework that shaped her meaning-making. Other people, facing the same set of random events, might have concluded some other meaning based on a different mental map, such as "It was a plot against me," "I messed up again," "The airlines are so poorly run these days," or "I was treated unfairly." Being aware of our mind maps is very important in our quest to fulfill our spiritual need for meaning in healthy ways.

Another common way that people, especially spiritual people, make meaning of life's random or unexpected events is to affirm that random events happen to teach us something. Random events—good or bad, but especially a painful turn of events—embody a lesson, something we are supposed to learn, maybe for the first time or maybe over and over again. Identifying this lesson is a powerful tool to discover the meaning of a life event. In this view, life is essentially a journey in personal self-discovery or self-realization. Life is full of painful lessons. With each lesson, we have an opportunity to grow, to become more aware, more mature, wiser, and more connected with the Divine. In so doing, we gain some good out of what may have initially seemed like a tragedy or a huge mistake.

Denise's experience also illustrates the truism that meanings are often discovered and/or refined more in retrospect than in the present moment. Often, after we pass through periods of suffering, mourning, and life-changing events, we look back on those earlier years with a new perspective (what I call a temporal perspective). Now, in retrospect, we can see the hand of God moving as a weaver through the fabric of our lives. Now, we can see that we were never really alone, just carried on the shoulders of an unseen divine companion. Meaning emerges when we look backwards, not forwards. So, we must remind ourselves, when we are staring at the meaninglessness of the present moment,

to not jump to conclusions,

to wait, and

to patiently let the meaning unfold in time.

Some of the mind maps by which we make meaning are psychological in nature. For example, comedian Rodney Dangerfield joked, "I don't get no respect!" For some, this phrase can become a map that explains their life. Events are interpreted again and again as additional examples of this perceived truism. Psychological maps can often be concisely summarized in phrases or short sentences or descriptive self-identifications, like "I am a loser" or "I can do no wrong."

Sometimes our mind maps are derived from our family, our tribe, our race, or our culture. Certain ideology-driven organizations, like cults or political or social movements, also offer mental maps for understanding life. particularly why bad things happen to good people. Often the go-to meaning that such organizations provide is some form of conspiracy theory: this bad or unexplained event happened

because of our enemies, or

because of big corporations, or

because of unknown pesticides or chemicals, or even

because of the Devil.

We must be careful about these meanings. They are simplistic and rarely hold up to a careful examination of the evidence.

Yes, our maps can collide, contradict each other, or become out of date. If our mental map is "I don't get no respect," what happens when we repeatedly get respect, even unmerited love? We need to always be open to new information, to learning from new experiences, testing, revising, and updating the stories we tell about life's random events. For most people, meaning-making is a work in progress.

One of the primary purposes of religion is to help us find meaning in our lives, but many religions do not help us find meaning as much as they offer us a predetermined meaning based on its revelation and teachings. Religion says, "Here is the meaning of life—of your life." Many people welcome such pre-established, traditional meanings that have stood the test of time. More egalitarian religions may give us just the tools, mind maps by which we ourselves can interpret our lives. For most religious people, these religious maps are helpful in making meaning.

It should be pointed out, however, that most religions are themselves based on the lived experiences of their founders. These great religious leaders were, after all, humans, albeit remarkable and spiritually mature individuals. As humans, they experienced the raw experiences of life just like us, including the randomness of life. Out of their own experiences, they fashioned meaning, meaning that was codified into stories, sacred writings, and eventually doctrines and institutions. These founders of religions, like us, had a need for meaning, perhaps even a much more intense need than most of us. Their need became a vehicle for revelation.

Finally, it should be noted that this basic need for meaning requires a good deal of discernment. Saying "It was meant to be" can reflect profound spiritual awareness. But it could also be a rationalization for an unwise or selfish choice. This statement could be a product of our own ego rather than a humble recognition of God's grace in our lives. So, how do we know the difference? By what criteria do we discern meaning in our lives? What tools do we employ to make sense out of life's random events? Perhaps the ultimate truth of any person's sense of meaning is seen only in the context of revelation, as an unfolding revelation of the Divine among us.

Reflection Questions and Activities

1. In your journal, write a story about the last time you said "It was meant to be." What was the context? Did your pronouncement prove true in the long run?
2. Watch the Oscar-winning movie *Forrest Gump* (1994). How does this movie wrestle with the meaning of random events? What are some other movies or novels that wrestle with the meaning or meaninglessness of random events?
3. What painful lessons has life taught you through unexpected, random events? Are you a better person as a result? If so, in what ways? Did these lessons give meaning to your life?
4. Reflect on this saying: "Maybe it is not meaning you are seeking but a relationship with God."
5. At this point in your life journey, can you describe, in no more than one hundred words, the meaning of life?

2

Trust

Trusting Life's Goodness amid Its Unpredictability

Life is unpredictable. We never know what tomorrow will bring—good fortune or misfortune, good luck or hardship. Human existence is this way—life is this way—even though we may pretend otherwise. Terms like luck, fortune, chance, and superstition reflect in everyday language this basic truth of the human condition. We know all too well that life is unpredictable. In short, stuff happens!

In this chapter we continue the focus on the random nature of life's events, but this time, in contrast to chapter 1, we explore it more on an emotional or behavioral level. looking at how we cope with the fears or sense of threat that arise in us due to life's unpredictable nature.

We long for certainty, foreknowledge of what is to come, a preview of how the dice will roll or who will win the Super Bowl next year, whether we will be hurt in love, or even when we will die. Lots of people make money off life's uncertainties, among them

casino owners,

prophets, and

astrologers.

Divining the future is as old as humanity. It is the practice or practices of seeking to foretell or foresee the future. It includes such common dynamics as using a Ouija board, reading tarot cards, and consulting with psychics.

A group of professional psychics called California Psychics has a radio ad pitching their services. It ends with the tagline "The joy of certainty."

While good things such as miracles can surprise us, we humans are programmed to be more sensitive to threats than blessings. Our two principle responses to potential threats are worrying and control. Worrying is a fairly passive activity. Taking control is more assertive, even aggressive. Yet, ultimately, we cannot worry enough or have enough control to rid life of its unpredictability.

Worrying does have its positive uses. It can motivate us to be prepared, to reduce the risks. Over the centuries, we humans have used science to control Mother Nature and improve our health. We use technology to track threats, viruses, and terrorists and improve safety on airplanes and automobiles. Our governments have created insurance programs, or "safety nets," and the police and the military exist in part to protect us and keep us safe. Even though we modern humans now control a good deal of life's dangers compared to our ancestors, our propensity to worry has not changed. Life is still basically unpredictable—or maybe the problem is in us.

Some would even argue we have *more* stuff to worry about these days than our grandparents did—threats like the climate crisis, terrorism, interpersonal traumas, and the damage that drugs and the internet might do to our children. These are new worries unique to our time. And despite all our "advances," millions of Americans still worry about putting food on the table and avoiding the gang violence down the street. Inevitably, the human journey, even in the best of times, includes losses, accidents, hardships, and ultimately death itself—the worry behind all worries. How should we cope with such basic unpredictability?

First, we must acknowledge that all of our human "fixes" have worked only partially. There is still a measure of unpredictability built into life. It is part of human existence. We need a more basic fix. We need something deeper, what I call a basic trust in the goodness of life. For this kind of trust, we need to reach beyond the plane of human activity into the realm of the spirit. But I am getting ahead of myself. Let's back up and explore worry and control a bit more because they illustrate the distortions and pitfalls of this process.

Traditionally, a religious method for coping with life's unpredictability is the use of ritual, particularly sacrifice and prayer. Sacrificing to the gods—something humans did for eons and still do in many cultures—operates on the assumption that giving up something or offering something to the gods will gain us favor and allow us to avoid misfortune. Religious rituals of all kinds are performed for essentially the same purpose: to influence the gods or God to bless us rather than curse us. When life seems most unpredictable, when our worry and anxiety rises to its highest levels, we turn to prayer and related rituals. It is no accident that prayer beads are called "worry beads."

There are all kind of prayers and styles of prayer. When done well, prayer connects us to the Divine and creates in us or reinforces in us a basic trust or faith in life's goodness. Temporarily, our anxiety is lessened. We take a spiritual deep breathe, relax, and lean into something greater than ourselves. For a few moments, then, our trust or faith in life's goodness is renewed. Prayer can also be treated as magic, as a wish list, as a form of manipulation, or as a performance. In these cases, praying only offers a temporary reprieve. A healthy prayer life that builds trust takes a lot of training and practice, more than most of us realize.

Besides religious rituals, many common secular rituals, like superstitions, knocking on wood, or crossing our fingers, serve the same purpose: to calm or release our anxieties. Such behaviors make us feel better, temporarily. And these rituals "work" just often enough to encourage us to try them again the next time life is scary. When our rituals are not successful, we may conclude that we performed the ritual incorrectly or insincerely. So, we decide to do it again, making sure

- our words are said just so,
- our attire is correct,
- our timing is exact, and
- our sincerity is evident.

Sometimes rituals, and even prayer, can be part of the problem, not the solution.

The other response to life's unpredictability, on a behavioral level, is controlling or overcontrolling behavior. We believe that we can protect our loved ones from life's dangers by monitoring, correcting, and hovering over them. Our controlling behavior is fueled by worry, of course, but overcontrolling also has its own momentum and can generalize to a temperament or personality style. Its intensity and pervasiveness can be fueled by exposure to worrisome risks and possible dangers, such as those that fill the news. Control does work, up to a point, prompting us to take measures to protect our families, but overcontrolling creates a lot of interpersonal and family problems. Worry and control can make us miserable.

We can understand how and why worry and control do work up to a point. Ultimately, these responses to life's unpredictability do not fix the problem. At best, they are tools to help us manage our anxiety, and often they are only temporary or partial solutions. To the extent that they are not successful, we remain vulnerable to well-meaning but immature leaders who offer reassurances, certainty, and denial in exchange for our loyalty to them or their cause or their religion. Their pitch is appealing. Who does not want reassurances in a time of fear, certainty in a world filled with uncertainty, or even denial in the face of a horror too great to bear?

Recognizing the pitfalls in these approaches to the challenges of life's unpredictability sets the stage for us to go deeper. Our spiritual need here is for a basic trust in life's goodness, or what I would call "faith," that can sustain us in times of trial and comfort us in times of sorrow. The only way to experience this deeper trust or faith is through the direct and authentic experience of the goodness of the Divine. It is not something we can think our way into, although thinking is important because faith can be blind and naïve. Ultimately, faith is built on our personal experience of God. We cannot manufacture, manipulate, or control when and how we will experience divine goodness. But we can place ourselves into positions or circumstances where we are more likely to experience life's goodness. Many of the spiritual needs described in this book, if fulfilled in healthy ways, will help us experience goodness and build our faith.

In addition, we can create and nurture a rich inner life for ourselves whereby we can connect on a regular basis with the goodness of the universe. Among the spiritual practices that can help us cultivate trust are various forms of contemplative prayer; forms of meditation that focus on being, not doing; participation in the arts, such as enjoying inspirational music; regular walks in nature; acts of charity; hearing stories about people of faith; singing or chanting trustful words and phrases; and practices particular to our culture or lifestyle.

Let's be clear that the opposite of basic trust or faith is fear, fear of life's randomnature and ultimately fear of suffering, loss, and death. Faith does not protect us from death or suffering.

Suffering is part of life.

Loss is a part of life.

Death is a part of life.

Faith does address the fear associated with these realities. Acting on faith, we are realistic about life's unpredictability but still choose to trust, not because we do not see life's risks but because we trust in an unseen loving God working on our behalf. We trust that Divine Love will create the best possible outcomes at the best possible time for our ultimate good. We trust because we have experienced firsthand this Loving Presence.

It is difficult for many people to affirm this kind of faith because their experience with human trust is so damaged and distorted. People with early experiences of distrust, conditional love, or inconsistent or absent parents have a harder time trusting in the goodness of life. This is understandable, but it can be overcome. For such people, faith has to be a choice, even a leap. And this choice must be made not just once but again and again, trusting the process. We develop trust by placing ourselves in positions where we can experience afresh the goodness of God and then waiting. Trust will return. Trust will not fail you. Keep your eyes open for signs of the return of trust.

- In time, we can draw on our inner well of trust.
- In time, we can draw trust from our trustworthy friends.
- In time, we can see the good things that are emerging.
- In time, we can see ways in which we have grown.
- In time, our sense of basic trust or faith in life's goodness will be restored and we will know again that all things work for good for those who walk in the path of faith.

Reflection Questions and Activities

1. How strong is your worrying and anxiety? Are you a control freak? How strong is your spiritual need for trust? Does your religion fully satisfy this need?
2. Where do you go or what do you do to connect with a sense of life's goodness?
3. A friend once said to me: "When I got to the proverbial end of my rope again, this time, I just let go." What do you do when you reach

the end of your rope? Did letting go of control or surrendering your worries become the first step in trusting the Divine?

4. Often, we experience life's goodness retrospectively. Share an example from your life of something that initially seemed a tragedy that you later came to see clearly as God's providence.
5. Reflect on Denise Levertov's poem "The Avowal" (available online). Does this poem capture your experience of basic trust or faith? What other poems or stories capture that experience for you?

3

Explanations

Searching for Answers to Life's Big Questions

LIFE IS PERPLEXING. WE have many questions, some of them unanswerable. Nevertheless, we look for answers. We long to know how and why something is the way it is. Young children ask questions from the simplest to the most profound: "Why is the sky blue?" "Where do we go when we die?" "Can earthworms see?" We are curious about the world around us. We ask questions.

Our need to ask questions is part of and overlaps with our quest for meaning, explored in chapter 1. This chapter focuses more on the cognitive dimension of the quest, the need to have answers to life's most perplexing questions.

Our need to ask questions, to search for explanations, is a distinctive human trait. We want to understand ourselves, our lived experience, and the world around us. This desire for answers is not exclusively a spiritual need. It is partly satisfied by science, philosophy, and our cultural heritage, but this need can never be fully satisfied without our taking the spiritual dimension into account because some questions, questions we inevitably ask, are unanswerable apart from a spiritual or religious perspective.

The human need to ask questions and seek answers has led to the development and evolution of science. We study, analyze, and experiment to order to answer our "why" questions, questions like "Why do humans fight so much?" "Why are there earthquakes?" or "Why did I get sick?"

Indeed, over the centuries science has come to answer many questions, questions that challenged our ancestors or whose previous answers became unsatisfactory. In previous ages and for many of us today, answers to the basic questions of human existence are religious answers. As the modern world has become more secular and informed by science, however, religious explanations have gotten less attention and become less satisfactory. Yet questions remain, and some questions go to the heart of our lives. They are the questions that are not easily studied by scientists, questions that require spiritual, theological, or philosophical answers. These are the questions that still haunt us, even, or maybe even more so, in the age of science.

The arts—theater, music, movies, literature, and the visual arts—are good avenues by which we humans wrestle with the questions surrounding our human condition. Storytelling is a good example, particularly origin stories. Storytelling can be informal. It can consist of family stories that answer questions like "Why is this place called Los Angeles?" "Where did our family come from?" or "Why are the Johnsons our enemies?" Storytelling can also take the form of theater, literature, or songs that capture and reflect humanity's search for explanations. Every culture also has its own myths and legends. Every culture has "creation stories" or origin stories—stories that explain why things are the way they are, where our people came from, how the world began, why people make war. We are storytelling, storymaking creatures. We humans use storytelling as a way of "explaining" life. So, one might argue that there are no explanations—only stories.

Religion was born out of humanity's quest to fulfill this need for explanations, particularly of what I call the "Big Questions." Over the centuries, religions have been successful to varying degrees at providing answers to these questions. The three or four major surviving religions in the world today likely represent the most enduring systematic attempts to answer these questions about human existence. The attempts are often formulated in doctrinal statements, like confessions of faith or theological decrees. Some Christian churches have made use of catechisms, which are doctrinal statements framed in a question-and-answer format that address the big questions of the founders' era and the agreed-upon answers. The problem, of course, is that the questions themselves are not always the same. They change, evolve over time, and they differ from culture to culture. Are we today asking the same questions that our ancestors did? Or are our questions just different versions of timeless questions? Many do not find the answers from earlier catechisms to be helpful because in part, the questions have changed.

What are the Big Questions for us today, life's most compelling questions? Here are some examples:

1. Where did humans come from?
2. Does humanity have a purpose, a destiny?
3. Is there a supreme being, and what is it like?
4. If there is a supreme being or a creator, what does it require of us?
5. What is real?
6. Is there another reality beyond what we can see and touch?
7. What is time? Where did it come from, and can we transcend it?
8. Is there an ultimate right and wrong? Is there an ultimate truth?
9. Why am I the way I am?
10. Why do bad things happen to good people?
11. What is wrong with humanity? Are humans good or evil?
12. Do we have a responsibility to our fellow human beings?
13. Are we alone in the universe? Are we humans unique?
14. Do humans have a soul?
15. Is there life after death?
16. What responsibility do we have for future generations and the natural world?

Questions such as these are specific to cultures and eras. However, the need for answers, the need to ask, and the need to search is universal; these topics are common to most times and places. These questions arise out of the universal experience of humanity, the lived experience of human beings.

We live in a time of rapid global change. Western civilization is becoming increasingly urbanized, pluralistic, secular, and interconnected as well as socially fragmented. In this context, religious people seem a little more lost today than in the past in the sense that many of the traditional cultural and answers to life's big questions no longer make sense the way they did for our grandparents. The need for explanations is still there, but there are fewer ready-made, commonly agreed-upon answers. So, without clear cultural guidance, a growing number of modern people are finding answers in "all the wrong places" or are grasping at inadequate or narrow answers.

How would you rate your need for explanations, your desire to ask and answer the big questions of life? Many people are restless until they find satisfying answers to these questions. Some are passionate about and even obsessed with finding the answers. These are probably the philosophers or theologians among us. Wrestling with these kinds of questions can be a pretty heady process. It is a process that intellectuals or aspiring academics often enjoy more than ordinary folks. For some of us, this process can seem to be a bit boring, the sin of idle speculation.

- Perhaps you are too practical or busy to give much thought to these larger issues.
- Perhaps you have your hands full just meeting the challenges of ordinary life.
- Perhaps you do not need any explanations or just have not thought much about these questions.

People may have a strong or a weak spiritual need for explanations that make sense. But everyone has some need in this area, a need that may surface more self-consciously in times of a crisis or life transition, which are times when we pause in our hectic lives to reflect, wonder, and question.

Another source of answers to life's Big Questions are the sacred scriptures, stories and doctrinal statements of organized religion. For example, Christian fundamentalists often treat the Bible like an "answer book." They say, "Everything anyone needs to know about human existence is in the Bible." Others look to doctrinal statements, such as confessions of faith or catechism (question-and-answer) statements of faith. These traditional answers may be fine for some universal questions. But it may also be that we modern humans are asking different questions or are framing questions differently from those asked and answered by our spiritual ancestors.

We have no built-in explanations of life. In the past, institutions such as the church, the state, or our culture have provided such explanations for us. Now, explanations are typically sought, found, or created on a more individual basis. So, if we hunger for explanations, we must do the work ourselves. Today's postmodern culture offers us a wide variety of satisfying and not so satisfying answers. It is a marketplace of ideas, some profound, some interesting, and some rather wacky. We must be wise consumers in our quest to fulfill this spiritual need.

Whether our questions are large or small, explanations are important. They shape who we are. Our most deeply held beliefs, whether they are clearly formed or vague, consciously verbalized or unconscious, shape who we are, how we relate to others, and our potential and limitations in life and in love. If these beliefs are largely unconscious, they are even more influential in our lives because they act without our conscious awareness and consent. Explanations that are identified, examined, and subject to occasional editing and revisions as our lives unfold become the framework upon which we build lives of meaning and purpose.

Because this spiritual need for explanations or answers to life's Big Questions is mostly a cognitive need, the ultimate criterion for an explanation should be "Does it make sense?" (not just "Does it feel good?"). So, every so often we must ask ourselves again, "Does this make any sense?" If an answer no longer makes sense or only partially makes sense, then we must go on a quest once again for a fuller or deeper understanding of life. That's actually okay. Maybe the very act of seeking is itself part of the answers we seek. Curiosity is a spiritual value! In the end, part of our spiritual journey may be learning that some questions are unanswerable this side of heaven and, in so doing, allowing ourselves to embrace the mystery that is life itself.

So, embrace the process, the search, and the quest, now and throughout your life. The answers are not nearly as important as the process. Learn, grow, explore, seek, learn. Be a seeker as a way of life. The search for answers to your big questions can be a life-long process. Maybe the truth we seek will not be found in any answers, however noble or well articulated, but in the process of seeking. Curiosity is a gift from the Creator.

Reflection Questions and Activities

1. Make your own list of the Big Questions in your life or use the list given above. How does your present religion or the religion of your childhood address each of these questions? You may have to consult some resources or interview a trusted religious professional. Try to keep the answers concise. Make your own catechism! Are these answers satisfying to you?
2. Name a movie, novel, or song that captures, for you, the essence of one of the big questions of life.

3. What do you think of the idea that both science and religion arise from our very basic spiritual need for explanations, for answers to our "why" questions?
4. Interview a scientist or philosopher and ask how they blend science and religion.
5. Spiritually, becoming an adult involves examining the answers that have been given to us as children and teenagers from our parents, our religion, and our culture and choosing them for our own, modifying them, or adopting different, more satisfying answers.

4

Transcendence

Finding Ways to Transcend Our Own Demise

Life is finite. Human life is limited; it is finite in many ways. We cannot be two places at once. We cannot fly. We cannot know everything. We cannot see the future or go backwards in time. Most of all, human life is finite in the sense that it will come to an end. All that we consider integral to our essence—our being, consciousness, values, history, accomplishments, and personality—will cease to exist. This too is part of the human condition.

Finitude actually covers more than death, but in this chapter I focus on death as an essential and foundational part of the human predicament and on our corresponding desire to transcend our own mortality in one way or another. This is the spiritual need for transcendence.

It is interesting to note that humans have several natural capacities to transcend time and space, even death. For example, *memories* transcend time in the sense that they bring reality, information, and feelings from the past into the present. *Imagination* is another human ability through which we transcend time and space. We can imagine what it was like in the past and create that past through story, embodied in literature and drama. We can imagine what the future might be like, anticipating joys and challenges, planning for the unpredictable, and rehearsing desired outcomes. Third, in *dreaming* we transcend time. Dreams can be terrifying or reassuring, insightful or mundane. But at their base, they are vehicles through which we can seemingly transcend space and time while we sleep. In some spiritual traditions, dreams are a vehicle for communicating with our deceased loved ones and/or with God. Dreaming allows us, however partially and temporarily, to transcend our finitude.

Besides drawing on these built-in capacities, we humans have also used science and technology to transcend death. Medical science has enabled us to live longer, to overcome diseases and bodily damage that would have doomed our ancestors. We are already able to replace worn-out body parts. Perhaps medical technology or artificial intelligence will enable us to transcend death itself, even if we live on only in a database somewhere.

In the meantime, death is still the ultimate form of finitude. This is our existential crisis. It is final, absolute; there is no negotiation with the Grim Reaper or even Father Time! Perhaps, if our life is miserable or filled with suffering, death will come

as a friend,

as a relief,

as a passage to a better life.

But for most people in the youthful or productive years of life, death is the enemy. It stands out there, just over the horizon, as the ultimate limit to life.

How do you and I deal with this limitation? For the most part, we ignore it, don't we? We deny its reality because if we thought about such things, we might fall into despair and a sense of futility—"Nothing matters because we are all going to die anyhow."

Yet psychologists and theologians suggest that even though we do not dwell on death very much, the realization of our own nonbeing is always just beneath the surface of our psyches. It is the background music to our life. Occasionally, a near-death experience or the actual loss of a loved one shocks us into a fuller realization of our finitude because all losses foreshadow our own loss of life. Yet, after our mourning time is over, we fall comfortably back into denial.

Some psychologists have argued that this ontological anxiety, and the mechanism of denial that sublimates it, is not a bad thing but actually powers most of the great accomplishments and vitalities of human life. The finite nature of life fuels our desire to make the most of our years while we can. It empowers us to love passionately,

to create beauty,

to achieve, and

to work hard "while the sun is high."

The very character of human life is fashioned by its limits. Can you imagine what human life would be like if it had no end?

So, we humans long for transcendence. We search for something or some way to transcend our finitude, even if only partially or metaphorically. Our various religious traditions all attempt to meet this need by positing an afterlife in one form or another. They each attempt to describe the nature and conditions of this eternity. Most describe a place that is good, a place free from suffering, a place of justice and peace, and a place filled with love. The presence of an afterlife can give us great comfort because we are assured that our demise is not final. We believe or hope that this earthly life is not the end to our existence. When we attend a funeral or memorial service, we are reminded of these convictions. We are reassured that the person or some essence of them does transcend death.

A more generalized and practical response of this need for transcendence is reflected in our desire to create a legacy. We want something of us, of our uniqueness, to live on, even if it is just our money or prized possessions. We want to be remembered. We want to pass on something of ourselves to the next generation.

Legacies take different forms. For most people, our children are our legacy. A part of us—our DNA, our hopes and dreams, our family name, our family business—will live on in our children.

They look a bit like us,

they act like us,

they value what we value, and

they may continue our unfinished work.

Family lineage is very important in human cultures around the world. Family can fulfill our need for transcendence; we see our children thriving and know that a part of us will live on in them. Our own life may be limited, but that of our family is not.

People seek to create a legacy in other ways. Some people want to be great national leaders and create a legacy of political accomplishments that historians will take note of and debate for years. Others may secure a place in the history books by setting a record as, for example, the first person to reach the South Pole or the first person to break the four-minute mile.Such people will not be forgotten. We all want the reassurance that we will be remembered long after we are gone. We can transcend our death through the collective memories of those who will follow.

Others want to discover something wonderful that will help the world be a better place; if they do, their name will live on forever in the history books as the discoverer or inventor of such and such. We award prizes for people who have contributed the most to humanity in certain areas of human endeavor. Earning such prizes is a way of transcending our death.

Others write a great novel, pen an epic poem, or direct a movie. Still others paint a masterpiece, compose a great symphony or design a building that will live on through the centuries as a tribute to their lives. They transcend their own death in the works of art they have left behind. A little bit of themselves, their uniqueness, and their creativity, will live on. Art is their legacy.

Fundraisers capitalize on our need for transcendence by offering us opportunities to transcend finitude. We can transcend our own death by having a building named after us or by contributing money that will advance the mission of a nonprofit organization. We can endow a building in the name of a deceased loved one, thus giving that person transcendence. These philanthropic activities have done much to promote medical science, education, and other endeavors—all because we need transcendence. Fortunate are the few who have the financial means to memorialize themselves or their loved ones in such ways.

Not everyone has the resources or opportunity to create a tangible legacy. Sometimes, a life well lived, one that is lived with compassion, love, integrity, and courage, transcends time. This is what eulogies focus on, right? We hope that the best parts of us are eternal.

As with the other spiritual needs, some unscrupulous people will play on our need for transcendence by offering to sell us false hope—

- by naming a star after a loved one,
- by promising to freeze our body until a cure can be found,
- by offering to place our name in the latest edition of *Who's Who*,
- by offering salvation through the purchase of an indulgence,

- by buying an outrageously expensive coffin for a loved one, or
- by offering to help us receive direct messages from our deceased loved one while in a trance state.

Others, nefarious leaders, do not want our money, just our absolute devotion and loyalty. They may want us to sacrifice ourselves for a cause in the assurance of eternal transcendence. Some of us are especially vulnerable to these offers, not just because we are gullible (perhaps we are) but because our spiritual need for transcendence is particularly strong, our earthly life is particularly miserable, or we are in despair over the loss of a dear one.

All of the ways we seek to fulfill this spiritual need for transcendence, whether they are overtly religious or not, involve embracing a larger perspective, the "big picture," so they are, in this sense, spiritual. Ultimately, transcendence is as much an attitude as any one act or pathway, an attitude that affirms that we will not be defined or limited by death.

In the episode of the television series called *Northern Exposure* titled "A-Hunting We Will Go," Ruth-Anne tries to turn seventy-five years old quietly, but young Ed Chigliak is struck by the profundity of her age and the potential loss of his friend. He throws her a party and gives her a gift of a jar of dirt. She discovers that the dirt is part of a grave site that he has set aside for her in a meadow with a beautiful mountain view. Upon visiting her future home for eternity, she has an idea—to take the opportunity to dance on her own grave. In joyful defiance, this elderly lady and this young Alaska Native man who wants to be a filmmaker dance on her future grave. The camera backs off, panning the scene, the beautiful vista of trees, mountains, and lakes, and the two human beings dancing on the ledge. In this moment, Ruth-Anne transcends death, not with a legacy or even a work-around but with joyful defiance.

Reflection Questions and Activities

1. Is our desire to surpass our limits a bad thing? Do you agree that our desire for transcendence has inspired advances in both medicine and science?
2. Name ten unhealthy ways that people try to satisfy their need for transcendence. Now list ten healthy ways. What criteria did you use to determine what constitutes healthy and unhealthy ways?

3. Is religion just our attempt to reassure ourselves that we will transcend death? Would religion exist without the human fear of nonbeing?
4. How do you hope you will be remembered in years to come? What do you want your legacy to be after your death?
5. What is eternal?

5

Wisdom

Knowing How to Respond to Life's Limitations

Life is finite. We experience our finitude in a variety of ways. We have ontological limitations, biological or genetic limitations, and limitations related to our social or economic status in the world. Our responses to each of these kinds of limits reflect varying degrees of ambiguity. Should we accept a limitation as the divine will, or do we strive to overcome it? So, the spiritual need here, in this second chapter focusing on finitude, is wisdom—not acceptance or courage but the wisdom to know the difference.

After forty-five years in clinical practice as a psychotherapist, I have concluded that this issue represents one of the most common, underlying sources of people's problems in life—sorting out what they are responsible for (and can change) and what they must learn to accept (because they cannot change it) and the various ambiguous mixes of these qualities. This issue is clearly part and parcel of the human condition.

In the 2016 film *Passengers*, Aurora Lane (Jennifer Lawrence's character) is prematurely woken up from her interstellar 120-year sleep and thus robbed of her promised new life on a distant Earth-like planet. Her first response is anger, even rage, as she tries to come up with a technological fix. In time, her anger gives way to acceptance, even joy, as she makes a new life for herself on the spaceship. Toward the end of her life, she reflects on her unexpected journey by recalling that a friend had advised her, before she left Earth, that she can't get so hung up on where you'd rather be that you forget to make the most of where you are. At the end of the movie, in her recorded message to her fellow travelers, she concludes that they had a beautiful life together. This is a spiritual-sounding lesson, for sure.

Other examples of our *ontological finitude* include our inability to be in two places at once, to fly, to know everything, and to see the future or go backwards in time. The choices we make or made are set in stone: I married John, not Jim; I chose this job, not that one. There are no do-overs! Time is a ruthless master. With each passing year, we age. There's nothing we can do about that. The common thread of these ontological limitations is that they are nonnegotiable. They are baked into the nature of existence in this universe and thus are part of the human condition.

Yet the scientific and technological advances of human civilization have made dents in even the seemingly absolute limits of ontological finitude. In a sense, we can be in two places at once when we are on the internet. Computers now enable us to have more knowledge at our fingertips than any human being before us has ever enjoyed. Artificial intelligence enables us to transcend our cognitive limitations. We can send missions to Mars or to the depths of the oceans. Using technology, we can probe the tiniest parts of the body or even the very structure of atoms. By doing these things, we have momentarily peeked through the cracks in the limitations of space and time.

The complex nature of finitude becomes even clearer in the second category of limitations, *biological limitations*. Most of us can draw on medical science and technology to alter or overcome what seemed like absolutes to our ancestors. Being born with a certain disability or even an undesirable trait is no longer always a life sentence. We can fix it. We can change it. But more than that, our attitude has changed. We celebrate people who overcome, who transcend the limits of physical disability or disease or injury. We do not tell them to accept their fate as God's will but encourage them to strive to claim a life for themselves, a life of normalcy even in the face of their limitation. In a sense, such people have transcended or "worked around" or surpassed their limits. These are the heroes among us who, although suffering terribly with pain or being limited in some way, still have a joyful and generous spirit. They remind us that even if we cannot change our biological limitations, we can choose an attitude of gratitude and joy in the midst of suffering.

But how do we determine when a limitation must be accepted and when the seeming "givens" of life can be overcome? For many, aging is a process of dealing with one limitation after another due to one small health decline after another. Medical science can help us overcome or compensate for each of these declines by replacing a knee joint, managing diabetes, or even having a facelift. We can defy or adjust to the limitations of an aging body. Yet there are limits. As we age, sooner or later we bump up against a limit we cannot change or should not change. A decline in health is inevitable, and if we deny it, we get in trouble, such as when we

- refuse to stop driving when we are a danger on the road,
- resist medical treatment, denying we have a serious illness, or
- don't get treatment because we think we would look weak or ugly.

In other words, there are times when we need to accept our limitations.

On the other end of the life cycle, today's young people wrestle with similar issues when they come of age. One of the developmental tasks of adolescence is coming to terms with one's body. Each person is a certain sex and a certain race. Are we okay with that? What if we do not like our appearance, our body type, and think we are too big, too small, too skinny, or too unattractive? How should a young person decide whether to accept their biological givens or, if resources are available, change some aspect of their body?

Who makes such decisions, and when? Suppose soon-to-be parents learn that their unborn child will probably be born mentally or physically handicapped. Should they

- accept this outcome as God's will for their lives, embrace it, receive it as a gift, and engage in building a beautiful life together;
- terminate the pregnancy and try again later;
- intervene medically, if possible, to get a healthy baby; or
- adopt a child instead of giving birth to one?

Is there a moral limit to these choices? Suppose the fetus has no medical deficits but the parents just want their child to have a certain hair color, nose size, or intellectual level? Where is the balance between fixing what can be fixed and accepting what has been given to them? These are difficult questions and reveal the complexity and even ambiguity of our need for wisdom.

Lastly, there is the category of finitude I call *social and economic limitations*. Each of us is born into and raised in a social and economic milieu—a caste, a nation, a clan, a culture, a family business. We may be born a slave or a refugee. For many millions of people around the world, even in the twenty-first century, these are ironclad limitations. These limitations may be understood as part of the divine order. Is poverty just the way things are? We may be told to make the best of it: "It will teach you character."

To the Western mind, social and economic status is not a given to be accepted but a condition to be overcome, if possible. We who are privileged to be born in a more open society believe that these social and economic limitations can be overcome or at least modified. We value choice in the face of finitude.

Modern societies go to great lengths to make choice possible. Even when we make a mistake, we can choose, say, to divorce John and marry Jim after all. We can determine how many children to have. We can change jobs or careers fairly easily in modern nations compared to our ancestors, who had limited work options. We can have children later in life than our ancestors did. Normally, there are no do-overs, but in some circumstances we can do something over, redo it, or at least mitigate our choices. We love a good story of redemption.

None of these categories of finitude—ontological limits, biological limits, and social and economic limits—is ironclad in today's world. One could view the advancement of human civilization as being about overcoming limits, advancing personal choice, and reducing the givens or at least putting a few cracks in the walls of finitude, all in the name of personal freedom. This is a far cry from the attitude of our religious ancestors, who believed that such limits are God's will for our lives and that happiness is to be found not in resisting finitude but in accepting it.

Modern life, with all of its technological advances and social freedoms, has made dealing with finitude complicated and ambiguous. It is challenging to know which limits need to be accepted and which can be changed or modified. Neither approach is more spiritual than the other. There is great spirituality to be found in accepting what cannot be changed *and* in having the courage to change what we can. So the spiritual need, the unique need, of the twenty-first century is not acceptance or courage but wisdom.

The Serenity Prayer is the second most widely recited prayer in the modern world. The key petition is "God, grant me the serenity to accept the things I cannot change, courage to change the things I can, and wisdom to know the difference." We need wisdom, but wisdom often must be earned through lived experiences. This is why wisdom is associated with age in most cultures. Wisdom involves having perspective, the perspective granted by well-lived years and by years of lessons learned. Wisdom as perspective can also be acquired through spirituality, by accessing the resources of a faith tradition. Various religious traditions elevate wisdom to the status of a god and value her guidance in human affairs. The Hebrew Bible has sacred writings called the wisdom literature. If you want a God who is practical, commonsensical, focused on happiness not salvation, and even a bit whimsical, wisdom is your spiritual pathway.

Life's limitations come to us in varying degrees of absoluteness. Some limitations must be accepted; others can be overcome with courage, hard work, ingenuity, and even a little technology. Much of our unhappiness in life comes from trying to change things that cannot be changed or shrinking from the challenge of changing what can or should be changed. The need, as the Serenity Prayer says, is to know the difference. To acquire the wisdom to know the difference, we must access spiritual resources. We must listen. We must seek. We must ask. We must study . . . and wisdom will find us.

Reflection Questions and Activities

1. What limitations have you experienced in each of the categories listed above (ontological, biological, and social and economic)? Describe how you determined whether to accept each limitation or overcome it.
2. Describe a story, a movie or a play that deals with the issue of finitude.
3. Who is the wisest person you know, someone who has deep, calm, insightful wisdom—an "old soul"? This is often an older person. Develop a list of questions and interview this person. How have they navigated finitude in their life?
4. The Serenity Prayer, which is central to the 12-step approach to recovery and sobriety, embodies the distinction between acceptance, courage, and wisdom. How is this issue central to the recovery from addiction?
5. In the West the practice of spiritual direction helps people to discern the wisdom and presence of God in their lives. Learn more about spiritual directors and their methods by contacting Spiritual Directors International. (https://www.sdicompanions.org).

6

Purpose

Celebrating Our Life Purpose or Organizing Principle

LIFE SEEMS WITHOUT PURPOSE. Sure, we can grow up and grow old, we can have children, and we can earn a living, but most of us at least occasionally wonder, "Is there more?" "Why was I born?" "Is there something special I am supposed to do?" Or if you are in your retirement years, like myself, you may wonder, "Did I do what I was supposed to do with my life?" "Did I fulfill my calling?" If so, then you can rest in peace; if not, then you walk on the edge of despair. A good deal of life, whether we are in our younger years or senior years or in-between years, is spent trying to identify our purpose. This hunger for purpose is part of the human condition.

There are lots of possible purposes in life. Certainly, raising a family, following in the family business, and being an honorable citizen are commonsense, even noble purposes and are truly satisfying for many people. Purpose, from a spiritual perspective, is a bit deeper. The core purpose of our life is *the organizing principle* of our lives. This is the principle (or principles) that shapes our life and how we spend our time and our days, and it is reflected in our values and, of course, our work. Hopefully, our work reflects the organizing principle of our life. It is wonderful when it does match, but sometimes our organizing life principle may be larger than any single job or jobs. This is like the difference between a mission statement and work.

A young man I will call Danny was an undisciplined, care-free person who enjoyed his friends, beer, and parties, getting by with as little effort as possible. After high school, he drifted a few more years, in and out of jobs, directionless, until he was "invited" by his father to enlist in the Marines. After an initial rough patch, he came to embrace Marine culture, norms, and values. He flourished as a person, mastering skills, taking pride in his hard work, and doing the job well, even becoming a leader. In time, he married and became a father. When I caught up with him a few years after he'd had his first child, he was considering whether he wanted to make the military his career. Reflecting on the difference the Marines had made in his life, he noted: "The Marines gave me a purpose, a life purpose . . . and it's a good purpose. I am protecting my family, my nation." He continued, "I now live a life of honor and duty, and discipline. In a sense, the Marines saved my life. I was headed in the wrong direction. The Marines gave me a purpose."

Perhaps you know similar stories of people who thrive only in an atmosphere with a clear and compelling purpose. For Danny, purpose was motivating, transformative, and larger than any given job he did in the Marines (and he did many). The Marines gave him a way of life, an organizing principle to his life, reflected in its norms, mission, and core values. Many organizations or dynamics can give our lives purpose. Religious organizations come to mind first, but all the great institutions of society offer us purpose. We even refer to nonprofits as "purpose-driven organizations."

Interestingly, a clear sense of purpose is one of the characteristics of people who live in "blue zones," communities across the globe that foster long, healthy lives. Having a purpose seems to be a universal, dare I say spiritual, need. Having a clear purpose rooted in a community is one component of human flourishing.

Organizations know the value of a clear mission statement that allows them to set priorities and move forward in an intentional way. Individuals can also benefit from having a mission statement—a concise one- or two-sentence statement that states their particular life purpose. But finding one's purpose or crafting a mission statement is harder than it sounds, especially in an age when we have so many choices. Some of us know early and easily what our life's work or mission is to be. We all know people like this—the ones who from an early age just knew that they were supposed to be a doctor, or an artist, or a soldier. Yet most of us do not have a clear idea of what the purpose of our life is to be when we are young. It requires some searching, or what religious people call "discernment."

Most of us determine our purpose in life partly by examining our gifts, interests, and passions. Those who have a gift for music, art, sports, or teaching conclude that this must be a sign that their mission in life is in the area in which they are most gifted. We assume that the Creator or at least our parents gave each of us certain gifts, talents, aptitudes, or abilities. We say of such people that they are "a natural" at such and such. Certainly, our gifts point us in the direction of our life's purpose. When we embrace our gifts, our purpose becomes what Joseph Campbell called our "bliss," something that enlivens us, captures our spirit and imagination.

For some of us, our sense of purpose only surfaces in our adult years, often in response to a life-changing or life-clarifying event. We stumble into our true calling when some unusual event occurs.

- We get a new job that really clicks, and we conclude, "Oh, this is what I was born to do."
- We fall in love and find in that love relationship the true purpose of our life.
- We experience a tragedy, and out of our pain and suffering, the purpose of our life becomes startlingly clear.

Stories of such people fill the TV talk shows and magazines. These are inspirational stories—especially for those of us who have trouble finding our life purpose.

People of faith say, "God has a plan for your life." This is a central precept of most religious traditions in the West. Western religions have a strong sense of the sovereignty of God, of destiny, and of history. They teach that God is active in history—in our personal history as well as the collective history of our species. Purpose is revealed in and lived out in history. This theological premise suggests that purpose is found or experienced not just when we examine the past and how we are made or gifted but also when we look forward. Purpose is revealed in our lived experience.

Another relevant religious term is "calling." People of faith may say that they have a calling. The implication is that this calling is from the Creator, who calls them to a particular vocation or way of life. Sometimes their calling comes to them as a vision or as a "sign" related to an unusual coincidence. Some churches believe that it is not just religious professionals who are called but, in a broader sense, that all of us are called to a vocation,

a way of life,

an organizing principle.

It should be pointed out that not all purposes are equally good. Some purposes are better than others, with "good" being defined generally based on cultural and moral values. Religion generally sanctions purposes that are religious, moral, and altruistic in nature or rooted in various scriptural teachings. But purpose does not have to fit into any of these categories. Certainly, Adolf Hitler had a strong sense of purpose, as have many other infamous or notorious people, past and present. For some people, revenge is an organizing principle in their lives. For still others, it is the acquisition of wealth. The spiritual need for purpose is universal. Everyone has—to a greater or lesser extent—a need for a sense of purpose. But the content or implementation of that purpose can vary widely. Some people are driven to do noble things, and others are driven to or unintentionally do evil things.

Some of us are so desperate for a sense of purpose that we are attracted to and easily bind ourselves to a larger organization, cause, religion, or even an admired person. We find their purpose to be captivating and appealing. It is common for people to do this to one degree or another, or at one time or another in their life. It is part of growing up and finding ourselves, isn't it? Putting aside the issue of whether the group purpose is inherently good or not so good, what is the impact on us of binding ourselves to a group purpose? Are we overidentifying with the group and thus allowing our self-worth to be too easily influenced by the group's success or failure? Have we suspended our own critical thinking skills in favor of groupthink? Have we found our unique purpose or just short-circuited our search? These are all important questions as we search for our own life purpose or organizing principle. They should guide us at every stage of our life.

Being committed to the wrong purpose or to an inherently evil purpose is like feeding our body spoiled food or polluted water; it does not ultimately satisfy our spiritual need for purpose. For most of us, purpose is not a one-time event or decision but an ongoing conversation between ourselves and our Higher Guide.

So, how do we know if our life's purpose is a good thing or not? What are the criteria for determining if our purpose is authentic and true? Finding one's calling involves at least three criteria:

1. an inner call that comes through self-examination and a "still small voice";
2. a confirming process by a larger reference group of trusted friends or community; and
3. an openness or flexibility to revisions or refinements in one's calling as the years and circumstances unfold.

Even though I know that our need for purpose can be abused and misused, I am continually surprised by how often great purposes or callings are altruistic in nature. It seems there is something deep within our souls that tends to tie altruism and purpose together. The most frequent and most noble purposes seem to involve activities that make the world a better place, that improve the human condition and/or leave a legacy of hope for the next generation. At a deep level, there must be a sense of obligation or responsibility we all feel toward the ongoing human experiment on planet Earth.

Finding, affirming, and celebrating our sense of purpose is one of the most important and essential of our spiritual needs. The healthiest kinds of purposes are those that affirm our gifts as a person, make a contribution to the greater good, give us joy, and are rooted in a life-affirming spiritual perspective.

Reflection Questions and Activities

1. What is your mission statement? Based on input from your family, religion, and culture, plus a careful examination of your own passions, gifts, and attributes, write a ten- to twenty-word mission statement for yourself.
2. View the 1998 movie *Simon Birch*, a story of a young man's search for and discovery of his purpose. What does this story teach you?
3. The Myers-Briggs Type Indicator and the Strong Interest Inventory are good vocational assessment instruments that can give you objective feedback on your gifts, talents, and aptitudes. Free versions are available online, but the best interpretive reports are available from the Myers-Briggs Company.
4. Seniors often have to reframe, redefine or re-invigorate their sense of purpose in light of their limited physical abilities and the waning of

the primary purposes of their adult years (work and family). Sustaining a strong sense of life purpose is essential for the vitality and mental health of seniors, who generally have much to offer the world. In your community, find some examples of organizations or programs that engage seniors in purpose-focused living.

5. In your journaling or in a quiet moment, reflect on this idea: maybe, for some of us, our life's purpose is not to *do* something but to *be* something.

7

Wonder

Seeing the Sacred in the Ordinary

LIFE IS REALLY VERY ordinary. From day to day, life is mostly filled with routine, hard work, and familiar problems and is maybe even a bit boring. We need some wonder, some majesty, some excitement, and some drama. We long for something extraordinary amid the ordinary. This is another aspect of the human condition, and it points to another of our spiritual needs: wonder. Wonder is a uniquely human experience.

Feeling a sense of wonder means being awed, inspired, and/or emotionally moved. Wonder is usually triggered by an event, an encounter that is perceived as sacred, mysterious, magical, or admirable, often something beautiful. Wonder usually catches us by surprise. It comes upon us as something serendipitous.

We humans have an innate capacity for wonder. This capacity is so uniquely human that we might say it is an essential characteristic of our species, as suggested by an alternative Latin name for our species, *Homo admirans*, literally "wondering man."

Nature, especially wild nature, gives us many opportunities for the experience of wonder. There is something about

being alone in the desert landscape on a starry night,

standing on a bluff overlooking the ocean at sunset,

watching an eagle sail on the air currents above canyons, or

observing a majestic rainbow.

Who among us, witnessing such scenes, can help but feel at least a tinge of wonder, awe, and humility? Over the eons, nature has shaped us humans to experience wonder. I wonder why.

Yet wonder can be experienced in many other places and ways. The birth of a child or the death of a loved one often evokes feelings of reverence. Sometimes special events or relationships unfold in ways that spark a sense of the sacred. Scientists talk about experiencing wonder or awe when they make a new discovery. Wonder is anything that makes us say "Wow!" or "Awesome!" But what exactly is wonder? It is inspired in part by beauty, in part by rarity, and in part by humility. Is not genuine wonder something more, too, something that can only be described as the creature standing in the presence of the Creator? Wonder is the very essence of spirituality and thus is foundational to most forms of religion.

Humans vary in their capacity for wonder. Some of us experience it more clearly and more often than others do. Yet, certainly, wonder is a universal or nearly universal human experience. If you agree, then think about these questions for a moment:

- Why do we humans have this capacity for wonder?
- What possible evolutionary advantage did such a capacity for wonder serve?
- Could our need for wonder be another footprint of the Creator upon our souls?

Knowing how foundational wonder is to spirituality, religious leaders try to nurture wonder. It is no accident that religious retreats are usually held in natural areas, where wonder abounds. Powerful spiritual experiences can occur at a summer camp. When we feel wonder, we feel small. We feel humble in comparison to the majesty and grandeur of the universe around us. Wonder reduces our innate pride and our claim of being self-sufficient. Wonder reminds us that planet Earth is a special place and that our simply being here is a gift. Wonder leads to gratitude.

Religious organizations try to create and recreate wonder on a regular basis so that our souls can be nurtured without our having to hike to a mountaintop on a weekly basis. For example, some religions build large and beautiful sanctuaries, filling the inner space with color, sounds, and smells that evoke awe within us. In more traditional modes of worship, the emphasis is upon creating an atmosphere of reverence and majesty. Great music, high ritual, and the drama of holy days create or were designed to create an experience of wonder. Where do you find wonder these days, especially if you do not attend religious services or if you attend worship in a more casual, contemporary style? Where do you experience reverence, the mystical, or the mysterious?

Our souls need wonder as much as our bodies need water and food, our minds need intellectual stimulation, and our psyches need self-esteem. If we do not have wonder in our life, where will we satisfy this need? The arts are a good source or context for wonder. Beauty often sparks wonder in us. The best artistic creations make us say, "Wow!" Consider Handel's *Messiah* or Michelangelo's Sistine Chapel,

or a majestic building,

a poetic story,

a powerful theatrical performance,

an artistic dance recital, or

an award-winning film.

What types of beauty make you say "Awesome?" Is the experience of wonder found only in the beautiful content of artistic creations, or can it also be found in the experience of creating art? In other words, is the act of creating also an experience of wonder? "Wow, look what came out of me!"

As I said, life is very ordinary most of the time. Religious practices try to bring the experience of wonder into our weekly or even daily lives, starting by noticing the special events of our live—births, deaths, tender moments, deep silences, dramatic moments, incredible beauty—and seeing the wonder present in these moments and celebrating them as sacred. The mystical traditions of the great world religions, at their best, have taken this one step further by teaching us to see the sacred not just in the extraordinary events of life but also in the ordinary stuff of life, not just on special occasions but also in all of the everyday experiences/events of our lives. The mystical traditions emphasize that wonder is there in every moment—but we do not always have the eyes to see it. By retraining our sight, sometimes through a rebirth of the heart, we now see the miracle or the presence of the Holy One where we failed to see it before. These spiritual traditions teach that the sacredness of life is in each flower, in each relationship, in each moment, no matter how ordinary or even boring it may seem. The spiritual perspective invites us to see beyond the material and the ordinary to the sacredness, the mystery, and the wonder embedded in the ordinary. In these traditions, wonder is in the moment, in every moment. Wonder is built into the very essence of life itself—if we have the eyes to see it and embrace it.

Wonder and miracles are tied together. Miracles are dramatic incidents of wonder. They are "wows" intensified a hundredfold. They are several exclamation points at the end of a sentence instead of just one. Miracles are signs or evidence of the Divine. I believe in miracles, so I am not knocking them here. Perhaps you have noticed how much we humans like miracles. We like to tell stories about miracles, and these stories seem to grow over time. It is like we have a hunger for miracles and this hunger is rooted in our deeper need for wonder.

We have a spiritual need for wonder. We need to see our lives peppered with miracles, and, in fact, they usually are. Yet it is one of the oddities of human nature that we fail to see most miracles but at the same time embellish small miracles into big miracles or create miracles out of our own need for drama and excitement. We focus on the big Hollywood miracles and miss the hundreds of quiet miracles that are hidden in the ordinary. This vulnerability allows magicians and demagogues of one form or another to use miracles as tools to manipulate, persuade, and control us. It is hard, isn't it, to know what is a genuine miracle and what is not.

Our struggle with wonder and miracles is complicated by the secular culture of the West, where there is less and less opportunity for experiencing wonder, mystery, and miracles. More and more of life is explained by science and materialism. We have been exposed to so much information via education and the media that few things really surprise us and cause us to wonder anymore. We are literally starved for wonder! So, we are tempted to manufacture wonder, to create it artificially through

dramatic stories,

the latest technological advance,

some display of magic, or

even the excitement of the latest breaking news.

While such creations do push our "wow" button, there is something terribly unsatisfying about inauthentic wonder. Our spiritual need is for genuine wonder, even as our body wants pure water and nourishing food. Genuine wonder happens by surprise, sometimes when we least expect it. It cannot be manufactured or manipulated. Wonder is a gift, freely given and humbly received.

Authentic wonder points to mystery. We cannot fully explain a wondrous event by scientific or even psychological analysis. Wonder is our response to being in the presence of the Sacred Mystery, the Holy Other. Mystery elicits in us wonder, in the sense of awe and of speculation. Wonder can also lead us to curiosity and inquiry, just as "wonder" in English is sometimes used in the phrase "I wonder why . . ." Wonder prompts us to seek to explain what is unexplainable. Maybe that was the evolutionary advantage of *Homo admirans*?

Wonder is the foundation of faith. Yet wonder in the world's spiritual traditions is experienced not just in religious events, places, and rites but also in things that are all around us. Wonder is a perspective, an attitude, and a set of eyes with which we see all of life and all of the ordinary moments of life as sacred. Maybe that is the greatest wonder of all: life itself. It is a wonder that we are here at all. And the second greatest wonder is consciousness, our innate capacity to be self-aware, to be awake, to reflect, and, of course, to wonder.

Our lives are measured not by how many breaths we take but by how many times our breath is taken away—by wonder. May our journey on Earth be filled with many breathless moments, moments that transform the ordinary into the extraordinary and fill our souls with the wonder of life itself.

Reflection Questions and Activities

1. Reflect on the last time you felt genuine wonder. Where were you, what happened, and who were you with? What made it wondrous to you? Sometimes wonder is a subjective thing. Expressing wonder in words loses something in the translation, but try to describe your experience of wonder.
2. What are some ways that people manufacture wonder or seek the experience of wonder in less than healthy ways? How about drug use? Risky adventures or dangerous behaviors? Or reliance on magic? What is the difference between a miracle and magic?
3. Does your church, denomination, or religion nurture your sense of wonder? How does this happen for you? How does it *not* happen for you? Is your church devoid of wonder, or does it try too hard to manufacture artificial experiences of wonder?

4. Does wonder happen more at certain ages? Are only children capable of wonder? Is it easier for a child to experience wonder than an adult? Why? Must adults give up such "childish ways" in favor of rationality and science?
5. Poets are especially skilled at capturing the experience of wonder. Read Mary Oliver's poem titled "Mysteries, Yes." What other poetry have you read that creates wonder in you or reminds you of wonder?

8

Hope

Nurturing Hope in the Midst of Suffering

LIFE IS FILLED WITH suffering. Most of us do not experience suffering all of the time, but it does happen. Into every life, some suffering comes—and for some of us, it is great suffering. This too is part of the human condition. We wish it were not so. In fact, we spend a good deal of time, particularly those of us who live in affluent societies, denying the inevitability of suffering. We tend to think that modern medicine and technology will fix it, like they fix so many things. But eventually, suffering arrives at our doorstep.

Suffering comes in many forms—physical suffering, mental suffering, and psychological suffering.

- People with a spinal cord injury sometimes live with great chronic pain. They suffer. Their loved ones also suffer with and for them.
- People who are prisoners of war may be tortured. They suffer during and after their imprisonment.
- Anyone who survives a life-threatening crisis may suffer from symptoms of post-traumatic stress disorder.
- Rape victims and other victims of violent crimesuffer.
- Survivors of natural disasters suffer psychologically and sometimes physically.
- Some people suffer with chronic illnesses and must endure surgery after surgery or treatment after treatment that result in only marginal improvement.

- People with serious and chronic mental illnesses suffer, as do those who must watch helplessly on the sidelines of their loved one's internal nightmare.
- People who have lost a loved one through death suffer. We sometimes term them "grief sufferers."
- People who live in war-torn or poor countries suffer hardships most Westerners cannot even imagine.

Yes, there are many kinds of suffering!

To some extent, suffering is in the eye of the beholder. We must not judge too quickly about who is and who is not suffering. What might be suffering to one individual might not be perceived as suffering by another. Almost all of us, unless we die in our sleep in good health, will live out the last years of our lives in chronic pain, with one or more disabilities, and/or alone. Suffering is inevitable in life.

We humans have a great capacity for suffering. Over our evolutionary history, we have endured famines, diseases, wars, and disasters. Perhaps one of the reasons we have achieved dominant status on this planet has been our ability to endure great hardships and bounce back. We have become a strong species in the evolutionary battle for the survival of the fittest. So, what helped us be so resilient? What helps us now in times of suffering?

Certainly, supportive friends, emotional comfort, and useful knowledge all help us, but isn't hope also an essential ingredient in times of suffering? We need hope. Hope is the confidence that things will get better—that this present suffering, as horrible as it may be, will not last forever.

Hope is based in part on facts, on knowledge. Here are some examples.

- The physician says that we will be better in time, so we are hopeful and can endure the present pain.
- Government leaders announce that the war will be over soon, so we have hope.
- We hear news about a new breakthrough, a new medication, a new treatment—and hope abounds.
- Reason tells us that a rescue party has been sent to look for us, so we wait patiently.

But hope is not dependent on facts alone. Sometimes the facts on the ground do not lead to hope. Our prognosis is poor. We are tapped out.

We are lost. And yet, we hope. We "hope against hope." How do we do it? Hope is not primarily a rational process; it is a spiritual process. In order to continue to hope, we must reach out beyond ourselves, beyond the mere human plane, to things unseen.

Religion is an institutional provider of hope. Hope is taught, encouraged, and promoted by most reputable religions. Helping people cope with suffering is one of the primary functions of religion. In a sense, suffering is the acid test for any religion, denomination, or church. Some people find out that in times of great suffering, their religion fails them. Their faith

fails to provide hope,

fails to provide comfort, and/or

fails to provide a reasonable explanation for why they suffer so.

People then drift away from their religion. Perhaps they find a new religious tradition, or they move away from organized religion altogether. For others, times of suffering lead to a greater depth of faith. Their religion works! They often become the best witnesses for their religion because they are the living proof that the truth of their religion works, at least for them. The proof is in the experience of suffering.

Religion or spirituality can provide hope in several ways. First, religion teaches us to trust in an unseen reality, a divine reality or God that is always capable of transforming hopeless events into a more positive result. Religion teaches us to believe in the possibility of miracles, even when miracles are not readily or predictably available. Furthermore, this divine reality is benevolent in nature. In theistic religions, the divine reality is called "God." God wants what is best for us, and thus we are able to hope even when a situation is hopeless. Hope is based in the belief that God has both the motivation (love) and the capacity(power) to influence events in this world. Therefore, hope is not rooted entirely in the known facts but is also grounded in a spiritual reality, a spiritual truth that transcends human reality.

Second, religion teaches that even without a miracle, suffering can be redemptive. Suffering is not necessarily meaningless but sometimes contributes to a greater good. This view is best represented in the Christian community, which chooses as its paradigm, in this regard, the suffering of Christ. Christ's suffering was not meaningless or random but fulfilled a larger, greater divine purpose: to provide for the salvation of humankind. Most Christian denominations have beliefs to this effect. Indeed, even in our everyday experience, we can affirm the simple principle that when suffering has a greater purpose, it is easier to endure.

Finally, when all else fails, when there are no miracles, when suffering may be clearly redemptive and especially when it is not, religion provides hope in an afterlife. Most religions affirm the reality of an afterlife where suffering "is no more," where justice prevails, and where loved ones are reunited. So, even when there is no hope in this life, many have hope in or hope for the life to come. The afterlife takes many forms and "conditions" depending on the religion, but most religions do affirm its importance. So, hope endures. Hope sustains us in this life in everyday ways, in times of suffering, in seeking a purpose in our suffering, and in the end by pointing us toward the life to come when our suffering will cease.

What is true in times of suffering—that we need hope—is also true in a lesser way from day to day and year to year. Don't we all have a basic, elementary hope that keeps us going in life? Human beings need hope. We are hope-needing and hope-making animals. Hope is a necessary part of the existential fabric of our lives. Without hope, there is only despair.

Yet our need for hope can be used, abused, or used against us by people with ulterior motives. First, there is such a thing as false hope. When we are in great pain, we can become desperate and are vulnerable to believing in false hope. We look for any promise, cure, or testimony, often from those who want to sell us something that might offer a miracle. Sometimes our need for hope can be quite desperate! Second, hope, particularly as it is understood in monotheistic religions, can create a kind of passivity. We are waiting for God to do something, to rescue us, and we fail to see what God is already doing for us or what more we could be doing to help ourselves. Hope must be an active hope, an engaged hope, an empowering hope.

Optimism and hope are similar concepts. They both affirm that life will get better. The optimism of people who are optimistic is based on available facts, on their personal philosophy, and on their assumption, via the power of positive thinking, that if they are optimistic they will help to create the positive outcome they desire. Optimism is a good thing. When we are optimistic, we are healthier, stronger, have more friends, and do, in subtle ways, help create the positive reality we long for. Rose-colored glasses are helpful—up to a point.

In similar ways, hope is also a good thing. When we are hope oriented, life goes better, despair is pushed aside, crises are weathered, and, in a mysterious way, hoping itself helps create what we need, not necessarily what we wish for. We must embrace an active hope. We must remember that even in the worst of circumstances, there is always a role we can play. There is always something we can do, even it is "only"

praying and meditating,
staying focused on God's goodness,
exercising our available choices, or
helping our fellow sufferers.

Unlike optimism, hope is based on a power that is greater than ourselves and our present circumstances, a power that can be accessed and mobilized to alter our present circumstances. We might say that hope has an "in spite of" quality to it. In spite of the facts, in spite of the prognosis, we hope. Our hope is rooted in God's goodness, not solely in the facts on the ground.

Hope has no guarantee attached to it. Even though we base our hope on God's goodness, we cannot control God. So, hope is interwoven with faith and trust. We trust in God. We trust in God's goodness. However, God cannot be controlled or dictated to. Sometimes what we receive is different from what we wished for. God has a way of seeing the larger perspective and nurturing an outcome that is best for us in the long run. So, our hope, our spiritually grounded hope, is not based on any specific act but on our trust in the loving nature of God and our faith that all things will work out for the good.

Hope is one of our most important spiritual needs, in part because, sooner or later, we will all be challenged by great suffering. In such times, we may reach beyond ourselves and embrace hope. But why wait? Deepening our spiritual walk now will prepare us for the inevitable hardships in life. Hope is as much about living a full and rich life now as it is about sustaining us in times of suffering.

Reflection Questions and Activities

1. What has enabled you to hope when there was no hope? Describe a time of great suffering in your life. What gave you hope? What is the source of your hope?

2. Research the origins and history of the popular song "We Shall Overcome." Is this not a song of hope? What other Black spirituals, born in the suffering of enslavement, are essentially about hope?
3. Do you find prayer helpful? What styles or ways of praying do you find most helpful in times of distress?
4. Explore and reflect on the dynamic of hope as depicted in one of these well-known movies: *Dr. Zhivago*, *West Side Story*, or *Shawshank Redemption*.
5. Does the very act of hoping help create the hoped-for reality? If so, in what ways?

9

Peace

Striving for an Inner Peace Rooted in Wholeness

We humans live lives full of conflict. We have social conflicts, psychological conflicts, and political conflicts. Conflict seems to be "a given" of the human condition. The resolution of conflict is peace. We long for peace. We need peace.

Peace, however, is a complex subject. There are various kinds of peace, including peace between nations, peace in the home, peace with God, and peace of mind. These four kinds of peace are interrelated. Peace in one area contributes to peace in the other dimensions of life. Yet peace in any dimension of life is tenuous and transitory—difficult to achieve and harder to sustain.

All the great religious or spiritual traditions promise peace in one form or another, mostly the peace that comes from following their prescribed religious practices and beliefs. But I think most religions of the world would also attest that inner peace is foundational to all the other kinds of peace. We must resolve our inner conflicts before we can see clearly how to resolve social and even international conflicts.

So, in this chapter, I focus on inner peace. Here are some of the types of inner conflict or stressors from which we may seek relief:

- At certain times in our lives, we want to be united with our family but also want to be independent from our family.
- When a traumatic event happens, we want to talk about it but resist doing so because it is so painful.

- When we pass into a new stage of life, we want to grow up but are afraid to.
- In times of crisis, we want to be brave in the face of danger but are afraid of harm and death.
- We desire revenge but believe in the need to forgive.
- We want more in life, but we want to be happy with what we have.
- We value our intellect, but our emotions lead us in a different direction.

Not all of our inner conflicts are clear or even conscious. Many are complicated by mixed or ambivalent feelings, such as an intimate relationship that could be described as a love-hate relationship. We want to be close to others but fear being swallowed up by them. These conflicts, because of their ambivalence, often reflect even deeper conflicts within our psyches.

Some inner conflicts are moral in flavor, a tension between what we *want* to do and what we *should* do. This dilemma is sometimes imagined as a war with our conscience between the angel and the devil sitting on our left and right shoulders, each whispering a conflicting message in one of our ears. There is probably a part of all of us that wants to do whatever we want even if it requires ignoring or breaking the law. Morals clash with needs.

Special focus must be given to the conflicts associated with addiction, which are becoming more common and more diverse in today's world. People struggling with an addiction are at war with themselves, with their temptations and cravings versus their desire to be healthy and free. For many, this is a daily struggle. They have willpower, and yet they are powerless. That's conflict!

Inner conflict is not always a bad thing. Conflict can spark creativity, synthesis, tolerance, and growth. Without conflict, we stagnate. Conflicts energize us. But some inner conflicts never seem to be resolved; they linger on for years, torturing the soul. In my view, the poison of conflict is not the conflict per se but the animosity, division, and even hate that is generated in the soul. So, we long for a peace that calms the restless soul, the wholeness that overcomes division.

Religion has focused considerable energy on helping us find inner peace. In one way or another, religion promises peace to its adherents.

- For some, peace comes from fulfilling the rules of their religion;
- for some, peace comes from forgiveness;

- for some, peace comes from living freely without strict rules;
- for some, peace will come only in the next life; and
- for some, peace comes only from surrendering to God's will.

The concept of peace with God is a distinctive type of inner peace. It assumes a monotheistic view of God and an absolute law or standard against which humans have failed. Some forms of Christianity suggest rather simply that all our inner conflicts will be resolved the moment we assent to faith in Christ. Salvation may be instantaneous, but wholeness rarely is. Believers often continue to struggle with their demons and a variety of conflicts. In fact, faith sometimes brings more conflict, not less. So, believers need to learn the ways of peace.

Many secular human activities are designed to assist us to find inner peace. Chief among these is modern psychotherapy, which basically does what religion used to do for most humans. Medical science also provides a kind of peace or wholeness. Political and social processes work on increasing or managing peace among humans. Education may also be thought of as a type of peace-building through knowledge.

Maybe we need to go deeper. Maybe we are seeking a deeper, more universal peace, a peace that is more than stress reduction, a peace that transcends religion. I think that this type of peace is more than the absence of conflict. Deep inner peace, particularly a peace grounded in spirituality, is a positive state of well-being and inner harmony that enables us to stop projecting our hate onto others. Authentic inner peace is interwoven with wholeness. This is one of our spiritual needs—the need for authentic inner peace. But how do we describe this deeper peace, the peace grounded in spirituality? Let me offer a couple of hints.

Alcoholics Anonymous often uses the term "serenity" to describe this type of peace. Serenity suggests the deep contentment that comes from giving up control, giving up compulsions, and surrendering one's destructive desires to a Higher Power. Serenity comes from giving up the conflict rather than trying to resolve the conflict. Or, serenity could be seen as a deep acceptance, including the acceptance that conflict is part of being human. In serenity, one realizes that conflict may in fact help us to be stronger,

grow,

know ourselves better,

define ourselves by our choices, and

increase our maturity and individuation toward becoming a fully whole person.

Many spiritual traditions also make a clear link between inner peace and transformation. Peace as a spiritual need is really about a kind of peace that transforms us, transforms our inner conflicts into harmony. This inner transformative work occurs when we integrate the opposite sides within us, when we recognize that each pole of our inner conflict represents a part of us, that each part or pole has strength and value, and that with the help of our Higher Power or a spiritual perspective we will be able to fashion a new wholeness, born of our opposites.

To use a metaphor from international conflict, this kind of peace is more than a ceasefire; it is a transformative process that turns enemies into friends. Similarly, inside of each of us, this peace-making process works to create "friends" out of the previously warring parts of ourselves. Peace rooted in spirituality has a transformative thrust that aims to turn conflict into harmony. This kind of peace, born of the unity of opposites, is sometimes referred to in religious traditions as atonement, or at-one-ment. It is attributed to divine power and grace. Yes, it is a gift, but it is also the result of hard work, hours of spiritual practice, and talking about, exploring, and dealing with our issues. This conversation occurs with and in the presence of a Higher Love. To be fully present with God, or connected to such Love, allows us to listen to our soul and our conscience, to detach from the flood of disinformation and propaganda, and to listen to our heart. This kind of peace transforms us, not in one miraculous event but day by day. Peace that is transformative is possible, and it is only possible as we connect to the spiritual world.

A client of mine, a wise older woman who had been assaulted and abused years earlier, shared that she struggled with her hatred for the abuser, hatred of herself for allowing it to happen, her desire for revenge, and her moral conviction that she must forgive, be fair, and not stoop to his level. She worked on her conflict for years in therapy and through her spiritual practices. She noted that a pivotal point came when she embraced two things. First, she understood that her angry desire to exact revenge or justice, to make him pay, was really God's problem, not hers. She cited the Bible verse "Vengeance is mine, I will repay, says the Lord" (Romans 12:19). She eventually was able to hand over to God her anger and her sense of being responsible for righting the scales of justice. She said, "God will secure justice and right the wrongs. I don't need to." She realized that her abuser would get his due, if not in this life, then in the next.

The second thing she learned was to empower herself, to see her anger as a strength, a protective strength that could transform her victimization. One of the manifestations of this transformation was her work with a support group for people victimized by sexual violence. She now describes herself as being at peace. It is a hard-won peace, a peace rooted in her vision of God and interwoven with the integration of her conflicting parts and thus her becoming a new person. Her story is not tidy or easy, but it is suggestive of the process of internal peace-making.

Peace, rooted in spirituality is not so much about getting right with God as it is about living into the presence of God and allowing that presence to transform us, integrating our inner conflicts and making us whole. This kind of peace is something we can experience now and as such is a sign of the "peaceable kingdom" to come.

Reflection Questions and Activities

1. How do you maintain inner peace in your daily life? What works for you?
2. Many relaxation or meditation podcasts are designed to be a tool to help us find deep relaxation and peace. Try one for thirty days. Journal daily regarding the process and the results.
3. What music do you find relaxing to listen to? Make a playlist of your most calming and peaceful music. Try listening to this music during appropriate times in the day and journal about your results.
4. Describe the principle inner conflicts that you wrestle with. In what sense are your inner conflicts manifestations of different parts of yourself? View the 2015 Pixar movie *Inside Out* to help you identify your inner parts. Can you identify a strength in each pole of the conflict?
5. Have you ever been on a silent retreat? What was that like for you? Was it peaceful or anxiety-producing or both? If you have never attended a silent retreat, try one as a way to cultivate inner peace.

10

Morality

Finding the Right Choice amid Life's Ambiguity

LIFE IS AMBIGUOUS. MANY times, it is not clear what is right or wrong or what the best course of action is. This ambiguity has increased in today's pluralistic, secular societies, where there is no consensus about what is good, not even on such things as social norms, gender roles, and ethical standards. It is more difficult than it used to be to determine in any given situation the right or wrong thing to do.

Certainly, some decisions in life are relatively easy to make. Other decisions, however, are confusing and complicated, involving conflicting needs, wishes, and expectations. Some decisions are even more difficult because we lack sufficient information and yet are being pressed to take action. Sometimes we end up making an educated guess, or, as the phrase goes, we "take our best shot." Life is not like a *Star Wars* movie, where the good guys and the bad guys are obvious and the moral choices are clear. Life is not that simple.

Decisions, decisions, decisions!

- Should I take this new job and uproot my family again?
- Should I marry this person, even though I do not fully love him?
- Should I testify against a loved one in court?
- Should I join the military?
- Should I have sexual relations?

- How should I discipline my child in this situation?
- Should I stop smoking?
- Which political perspective is right for me? For my family or my nation?
- Should I place my mother in a nursing home?
- Would my sister wish to live on life support machines?

I was often surprised by the number of people who came to my counseling office over the years wondering, "What is the right thing to do?" Yes, they had their personal preferences, needs, and wishes, but apart from all that, many people seemed to be genuinely and sincerely asking, "But is it the *right* thing to do?" There is something deep within us all that needs to know right from wrong. We have an instinctual sense of fairness, justice, and rightness. Children often complain, "It's not fair," as if there is some inherent sense of fairness that we are all born with. So, when the difficult decisions of our lives press upon us, most of us reach out for guidance. We would like someone to tell us what the right thing to do is.

Our need for moral guidance has been addressed in the past and is being addressed today by social forces. Governments have laws that tell us what is right and wrong. If there is a dispute, courts determine what is fair and just. We could hardly function as a civilized society without a legal code to govern our relationships and our obligations and duties to one another. Our culture, our family, and our various reference groups also guide us morally. Each culture, institution, or social group we participate in has spoken and unspoken social norms, expectations, and values that condition and shape our choices. Lots of people and social organizations tell us, directly or indirectly, what is right and wrong, attempting to shape our values and control our behavior.

So, our need for moral guidance is partly satisfied by our social institutions. For many of us, this guidance may be all we need or want. For others, and for all of us to a lesser degree, this same need is also a spiritual need. No set of human-made rules or courts of law can satisfy all of the infinite variations of moral dilemmas we face. Life is complicated and confusing. Legal regulations and social expectations give us some guidance, but we long for a more certain, a more absolute authority.

Sometimes we turn to a moral code to guide us in making difficult decisions. Most religions provide their believers with a moral code, a system of rules in one form or another that spells out right and wrong. Moral codes that derive from religion typically include rules that govern human relationships and rules about religious rites and rituals. In many religions, particularly Western monotheistic religions, the two sets of rules are interrelated. How one behaves toward God is interwoven with how one behaves or should behave toward one's fellow human beings. Knowing right from wrong has both a horizontal and a vertical dimension, we might say.

Religion also does something more than any mere social institution or government can do. Religions anchor their moral codes in a higher authority. Moral rules are not just fashioned by humans. They are also rooted in and derived from revelation. This issue of authority in moral matters is another aspect of our spiritual need for a moral compass. We have noticed that morality and social conduct are somewhat relative—they vary from group to group, from organization to organization, and even from society to society. As a result, many of us long not just for a moral compass but for a moral compass rooted in a larger truth, some higher authority. Is there a universal standard of right and wrong? Is there a moral code that comes with the authority of the Creator? Is there a moral code regulated by a divine judge to whom we will answer?

There are two broad dangers related to moral codes. First, some people have no formal moral code at all and tend to make decisions unconsciously, without critical reflection or thinking through the consequences. They tend to do what "feels right." Their decisions reflect the pressures and expectations of friends, family, and the prevailing values of their culture and the media. Further, they tend to make decisions, like all of us, rather quickly, without thoughtful reflection, based on whatever seems easiest or quickest and satisfies their or their family's perceived needs.

In this age of secularism and moral relativism, it is challenging to describe, much less feel certain about, one's own personal morality. Without a moral code of conduct of some kind, we can be adrift on a sea of indecision, unable to make choices when the variables are ambiguous and we are tossed about by the waves of changing social norms. Now more than ever, we humans really need a reasonable, thoughtful, and informed moral code of conduct. Without it, we are vulnerable to the promises of religious and political demigods who tell us what to think and how to act.

The second danger is a moral code that is too strict, too comprehensive and detailed, too black and white. Such moral codes try to regulate every aspect of our lives, from what we should wear and eat to relationships with the opposite gender to family life, politics, and work life. Such systems are set up or evolve because we are anxious and are trying to do the right thing, trying to appease what appears to us be a random God, so we detail everything out. Such codes

discourage critical thinking,

discourage situational ethics,

tend toward perfectionism and absolutism, and

tend to see the world in terms of either/or or us versus them.

Such attempts to create overly detailed and comprehensive moral codes ultimately do not work because such codes cannot imagine every possible situation. They can also become a tool of oppression. Nevertheless, strict and comprehensive moral codes are appealing. They offer certainty and rootedness in a world where the ground is always shifting.

So, what is a healthy moral code? Probably the healthiest moral code is one based on firm principles rather than rigid rules, principles that can be applied in ways appropriate for the situation, principles based both on spiritual teachings and on experience with cultural norms and standards. It is up to each of us, in each unique situation, to apply the principles appropriately. Having clear principles is better than having no moral code—it gives us some guidance as long as the principles are clear, and it is also better than a rigid moral code that is inflexible and judgmental.

But let's go deeper by asking this question: What is a *spiritual* perspective on morality, in contrast to a religious viewpoint? A spiritual perspective would ask a larger question: "What is the greater good in this situation—not what is right or wrong but the greater good?" A spiritual perspective, in other words, stands apart or above the moral battles between right and wrong or between two warring foes. God does not take sides in human disputes. God sees all of humanity as one family and therefore challenges us to find a solution, a choice that augments the greater good of all humans. Often, this spiritual perspective is also a temporal perspective, a perspective the considers the long-term effects of a given moral choice. Is this choice going to benefit us—all of us—twenty or fifty years from now? Similarly, in the realm of personal moral choices, God prompts us to think not in terms of right versus wrong but in terms of a win-win choice, one that promotes the greater good for all. Sometimes that choice might be one option, sometimes another option, but often it is a new third option that had not been previously identified, an option that takes into account everyone's good and has a perspective that extends beyond the present.

Traditional monotheistic religions understood God as moralistic, concerned about right and wrong. A spiritual perspective, at least spirituality as it is viewed in the twenty-first century, offers us a vision of God as above morality. Yes, some moral decisions individually and collectively have a clear, unambiguous right choice, but many more decisions are complicated, messy, divisive, and may have unforeseen consequences. In these situations, our Higher Guide prompts us to stand outside of a right-versus-wrong dichotomy, outside partisan politics, outside of the present battle, and find the greater good, the good that helps all parties and all of God's children. This is not about a moral code that leads to one choice or another but about a perspective, a tool we can use to navigate our moral dilemmas.

Life is ambiguous. Even with a healthy moral code or a spiritual perspective, life is still ambiguous. Moral choices are not easy. But if we can embrace the ambiguity and rely on our innate desire to do the right thing and our trust in our Higher Guide, the best choices will emerge. Remember in all situations that we do have a divine companion, a wise and courageous friend, who is always present with us and in us and will transform all of our decisions, our good ones and our not so good ones, into decisions that are good for all.

Reflection Questions and Activities

1. Journal about a difficult moral dilemma in your life. Describe the process you went through in making your decision. What guideposts helped you?
2. View the Oscar-winning movie *Schindler's List* (1993). Put yourself inside Oskar Schindler's context—his culture, history, family, and personality. How did he determine the right thing to do?
3. Write out ten rules or ten principles that guide you, whether unconsciously or consciously. Where did you derive these principles? How rigid or flexible is your moral code? How well does this system work for you?

4. Describe your moral compass. How does it guide you to determine what is the right thing to do? How do you access your moral compass? What clouds it from view or gives you false readings?
5. Look up the United Nations' Universal Declaration of Human Rights. Do you think it is a reasonable attempt to establish a global moral code for all of humanity? What rights or topics would you add to it?

11

Oneness

Seeking a Mystical Oneness with the Universe

Life is lonely. Ultimately, we are born, we live, and we die alone. Most of us are reasonably successful at making connections with others—friends and family—and finding community. Yet an existential loneliness is a part of the human condition. As a result, we humans have a spiritual need for what I call "mystical oneness," which is a unity that transcends time and place, a unity that transcends individuality.

I met a woman named Latisha when I was a hospital chaplain. Latisha was raised in a strict religious home but as a teenager rebelled against the morality and restrictions of her parents. During those years, she was fond of going out to raves, often secretly or against her parents' wishes. For Latisha, the raves—where she danced with frantic energy to the beat of loud music and pulsing lights, sometimes using alcohol or drugs—were very intoxicating. Things went from bad to worse at home. She eventually left her family home and tried to make it on her own, without a high school education. She drifted from job to job, place to place, and man to man. Often what little money she had was spent on drugs. Years later, when I met Latisha, she had just given birth to her first child. Being a mom was huge in her life. It gave her a purpose and significance but something else, too. After breastfeeding her infant one day, she shared that nursing her infant reminded her of the oneness she had experienced on the dance floor when she was going to raves. She connected the dots. I took it a step further and framed her last fifteen years as a spiritual quest (not as psychological maladjustment or social rebellion) and, ever so gently, suggested that maybe she was not so different from her parents and their religion as she thought. Were these different expressions of the same spiritual need?

Here are some manifestations of our need for oneness:

- Psychoanalytic theories suggest that we humans have an unconscious longing to return to the womb, to an existence characterized by the mystical oneness before our sense of individuality, or separateness, emerged during our first few years of life.
- Sexual relations between two loving people can be routine, exciting, romantic, erotic, and at times transcending. Sexual intercourse can lead to an experience of oneness, just for a few moments—a merging of two bodies and souls.
- People who have been through a traumatic event together or who have suffered together for years often come through such trials with a deep sense of oneness, a group bonding.
- The experience of participating in a mass movement—such as a religious service, a political rally, or a social justice movement—often creates a sense of unity. The emotional intensity of such movements, when people are united by the cause or their adoration of the leader, enable people to experience deep connections with one another, a sense of oneness that transcends their individuality.
- Some religious traditions promote spiritual practices that facilitate this experience of mystical oneness with one another, with God, with life, and even with the cosmos. In such religious traditions, the individual's afterlife is likened to a droplet of water flowing into and merging with the ocean, where all is one. Individuality has dissolved away into a mystical oneness or a return to the oneness from which we all came.

Religion has traditionally tried to meet our need for oneness to various degrees, from a sense of community with others to mystical oneness with the Divine. Religious congregations provide community, a place for its members to belong and to give and receive support and love. Religion also facilitates ways for its adherents to connect with God, even to be at one with the Divine. This is one of the primary functions of most religions. The pathways to this oneness include prayer, sacraments, chanting, singing, fasting, and even suffering as the founder suffered. There are also special times—retreats or revivals or pilgrimages—that offer opportunities for more intense experiences.

Mystics and monks meditate and pray for long periods of time. Many understand that what they are trying to achieve is oneness with the Divine Consciousness. They believe that the boundaries between themselves and the spiritual world melt away. They and God are one, at least for a moment or two. This experience of mystical oneness is powerful, even transformative. Often people return from such primary religious experiences enlightened, with new insights and a new sense of purpose.

A more energized pathway to oneness with God is found in Pentecostal or Spirit-filled Christian congregations, in which worshippers often get caught up in various charismatic gifts—tongues, prophecy, miracles, and healings—and in these moments feel that the Holy Spirit is dwelling within them. They experience union with the power and presence of the living Christ and with each other.

Most religious traditions outside of the West make physical activity like dance much more a part of worship than Westerners do. People dance together for celebration and for mourning. The pulsing rhythm of music, drums, light, and darkness sometimes creates a trance-like condition, not unlike what happens at a rave. The modern age of individualism is really quite foreign to our human nature and may explain our pressing need to experience oneness.

In some cultures, the use of mind-altering chemicals is another pathway to facilitate this sense of oneness with others and/or the universe. Various Indigenous cultures have used plants and herbs as an agent of worship, inducing a "vision state" or a meditative state in which a person can see visions and receive messages from the realm of the spirit.

The human spiritual need for mystical oneness is transformative but also dangerous. It can be life-enhancing, but it can also be destructive, depending on the character of the oneness, the timing, and the intensity. Many people experience a oneness in tribal-like activities, such as modern mass movements—from political rallies to religious cults to revolutionary protests or even to the mass crowds of sporting events. Charismatic leaders or the media rev up the crowd with excitement, drama, divisiveness, paranoia, and wild promises. All of the major evil isms of our era—communism, nationalism, fascism—have been promoted in mass rallies. Mass rallies or movements lure us by their promise of a mystic oneness.

One of the most dangerous aspects of mass movements happens when group consciousness or oneness reinforces the mindset of "us versus them." A nefarious leader can persuade their followers that "them" is a danger to "us." So, each movement has

their enemies,
their others,
their opposition, and
their rivals.

The irony here is that this lure of oneness may lead us to participate in movements that ultimately divide us. In a sense, the experience of mystical oneness is a bit like drug addiction; the initial experience is a high, but the long-term effects are destructive, the very antithesis of the spiritual oneness we were seeking. The leaders of such mass movements or cults, however charismatic they may be, are false prophets. They hijack our spiritual need for oneness (and purpose, significance, etc.) and use it to build their totalitarian empire.

Is there such a thing as too much oneness? Some people approach their family and love relationships with an overly sharp need for oneness in the form of fusion or what family therapists call "enmeshment." People have differing needs for unity and separateness in family relationships. Relationships can be soured by too much togetherness as much as by too much estrangement. The healthiest kind of oneness, at least in human love relationships, is a balance that fosters both closeness and separation, individuation and unity, sacrificial love and self-love.

A wise Catholic monk who had spent years in monastic life shared with me an image of oneness that seemed healthy and positive. He told me that spiritual oneness is not the oneness of sameness but the oneness of a symphony orchestra. It is the blending of sounds, each from a unique and varied instrument, to create something beautiful that is greater than the sum of its parts. This is an apt image for a healthy kind of oneness that is at the core of our spiritual need for mystical union.

How can we acknowledge our deep and passionate need for oneness? Can we find ways to fulfill this need without violating our own individuality, moral standards, and psychological stability? In general, the answer to this question is found in timing and wholeness.

1. Spiritual "peak experiences" are healthiest when they do not dominate our life. Experiences of mystical oneness should be rare events, not events that happen every day or even every week. We are not meant to live on the mountaintop, only to visit it occasionally.
2. The experience of oneness needs to be balanced with and honor our individuality and dignity. If we choose to submerge our individuality with the Divine or a group, the union should be brief and empowering, not diminishing and enslaving.
3. Spiritual peak experiences that are life-enhancing have practical consequences. They make us better people after the experience is finished. The inner world of our spirit should empower us to do justice, love our neighbors, and live authentically.

A final observation is that the spiritual oneness we seek may not be found in any single peak experience but instead in a perspective on life. Recent advances in cosmology, space exploration, DNA research, ecosystem studies, and quantum physics remind us that we are *already* one with the universe in profound and mysterious ways.

- The water we drink today is the same water that has circulated into and out of the Earth and has been drunk by millions of people and creatures across this planet for five billion years.
- We owe our very existence to the trees and plants that recycle our oxygen.
- The atoms in our body were born in the fiery furnaces of stars that lived and died eons ago.
- Our basic DNA structure is the same as that of every living creature on this planet.
- At the subatomic level, all matter is the same—energy—and is linked to all other matter in the universe, both near and far away.

Whether we realize it or not (and most the time we are too busy to be so fully aware), we are already one with the universe. Maybe our spiritual need or longing for oneness only reflects this deep, fundamental reality. Our longing for oneness is therefore best achieved through various spiritual practices that enable us to see this deeper reality.

Reflection Questions and Activities

1. Journal about when and where you have you experienced mystical oneness. What was the context? Describe it in your own words. How has it changed your life, for better or for worse?
2. Do you know people who used drugs to gain spiritual or mystical experiences? How did that work out for them?
3. Look up Lebanese-American writer and poet Kahlil Gibran's poem "Fear." Reflect on its perspective on oneness. How do you respond to his metaphor? Can we have an encounter with the Divine and not lose our individuality?
4. Does the modern electronic age increase the power of tribalism and its implicit lure of oneness? Where do you see the dangers of tribalism in our world today?
5. Identify a living spiritual master of a religion of your choice and sign up for a workshop or go interview them. Learn what they have to teach you about mystical oneness and the tools to achieve and manage it.

12

Gratitude

Embracing Gratitude as an Attitude

HUMANS ARE THE DOMINANT life form on earth. This is a fact of human existence, a part of the human condition. We use other animals and many of Earth's natural resources to sustain our lives and advance human civilization. We have become accustomed, even feel entitled, to treating the natural world as if it is here to serve us. And yet we humans long to connect to the natural world. Many of us know at a deep, instinctual level that we belong to nature. When we are in the presence of nature, we feel humble. We feel grateful. We might say gratitude is in our DNA.

Gratitude is an essential dynamic in social interactions. Human relationships are built on an unspoken system of credits and debits.

- We receive gifts.
- We do favors for one another.
- We are invited to dinner.
- We borrow tools.
- We give gifts.

It is important that we say thank you. This helps maintain social harmony, not only to satisfy our debits but also because gratitude begets generosity. Gratitude helps the giver and the receiver feel appreciated. Gestures of gratitude help solidify relationships. Gratitude builds cooperation and community.

Why do we feel the need to say thank you? Is it simply guilt on our part? Is it just a social nicety? Or is there something more, something deep within our souls that needs to give thanks?

Americans celebrate the national holiday of Thanksgiving, which was established to foster gratitude. Its architects thought that gratitude was essential for the moral and spiritual fabric of a nation. They felt that Americans have much to be thankful for and that the practice of gratitude was good for our moral character.

Those of us who grew up in religious homes may remember saying grace before the evening meal, a brief pause to acknowledge the Provider and those humans who grew, harvested, and prepared our food, such as farmers and cooks. Saying grace is a difficult spiritual practice to maintain in an age of fast food, complicated family schedules, and ever-present electronic intrusions into our homes. But, I ask you, did it fulfill a need that now goes unfulfilled?

We who live in urban settings are several steps removed from the process of food preparation or the sacrifices that animals make for our survival or the essential role that trees play in providing oxygen. These are just a couple of the silent and unseen gifts we take for granted. Technology has advanced so much that we can purchase our essentials without seeing or even understanding the cost to the natural world. Who needs nature? Why should we say thank you?

Not only do we take these necessities for granted, but worse still, we moderns, particularly we affluent moderns, have a growing sense of entitlement—the opposite of gratitude. This means we may become more complainers than prayers. And that attitude of entitlement spills over into the arena of human relations when we think that other people are here to serve us. This attitude is reinforced by affluence; the wealthier we become, the more we tend to feel entitled. Entitlement poisons social harmony and inhibits generosity. The acquisition of wealth, the goal of the American dream, has its perils!

It is very difficult for the rich, famous, and powerful to embrace gratitude. They are used to having it all. Many of them are used to earning everything they have, to being self-sufficient and independent. With a twinkle in his eye, Jesus noted that it is more difficult for a camel to go through the eye of a needle than it is for a rich person to enter the kingdom of heaven. Gratitude is central to all of the great religious traditions of the world, but gratitude is hard to embrace when you have never been without,

hard to embrace when you have limited experience asking for or receiving help,

hard to embrace in this age of self-promotion, and

hard to embrace in a culture that overvalues work and self-sufficiency.

So, let's go to a deeper spiritual reality. Gratitude can be more than a response to particular acts of generosity. Gratitude can also be an *attitude*.

- Gratitude can be an attitude toward life in which we see life as a gift.
- Gratitude as an attitude sees beauty, nature, friends and family, our health, our nation, our possessions, and even the preciousness of each moment as gifts.
- Gratitude is a positive and optimistic orientation of looking at what we have, not at what we do not have. It is inherently uplifting.
- Gratitude as an attitude changes us. It transforms us from a state of resentment and entitlement to a state of optimism and joy.

Gratitude as an attitude supports us in times of suffering and hardship. To be a grateful person when life is not going well is beyond the ordinary understanding of gratitude. This calls for another level of gratitude, a gratitude rooted in spirituality.

A young friend of mine, who did not have an easy time in life, was fond of saying, "Things could be worse." Often this was a simple, dismissive response, at times even a denial of her painful reality. It also reflected a certain wisdom, taking a wider perspective that considered other possible hardships, In comparing her situation to that of others, she was able to embrace a measure of gratitude. Her refrain reflected a broader perspective, essentially a spiritual perspective, that is the foundation of an attitude of gratitude. This kind of gratitude has an "in spite of" quality to it. In spite of the fact that things are not going well,

we will be thankful.

we will not focus on the negative, letting resentment consume us, and

we will choose to focus on what we can be thankful for.

This kind of gratitude, gratitude as an attitude, is rooted in a spiritual perspective. To embrace this kind of gratitude, we must think beyond the human plane. Seeing life as a gift requires that we believe that there is a gift-giver, a Creator, a Provider. We are not entitled to life. We do not deserve life. Life is a gift, given freely. To be grateful, then, we must let go of our self-sufficiency and independence, at least for a few moments, and say thank you for the gift of being alive.

Embracing gratitude as an attitude toward life is not easy. Most of us have felt this way on occasion. We often feel this way after a near-death experience or a tragedy that was avoided or a time when we had to do without. In the aftermath of such experiences, we appreciate life all the more, don't we? Now we appreciate the health we *do* have, the possessions and relationships we *do* have. We may even appreciate each moment, each day that is given to us anew each morning—and our healthy body or our loved one that we could so easily not have. Yet there is something about the human condition that makes it difficult for us to sustain gratitude. Persons of great spirituality can do it, but most of us ordinary folks find that

- all too soon, we start to take things for granted again,
- all too soon, we start to think negatively again,
- all too soon, we start focusing on what we don't have instead of what we do have, and
- all too soon, our gratitude is drowned out by the difficulties in our life.

The great spiritual traditions of this world all affirm that life is a gift. To get to the point where gratitude becomes an attitude toward life, and thereby a way of life, requires spiritual practices of one kind of another. Most of us cannot reach this deeper level of gratitude without some support, such as a community or a spiritual guide or companion.

Certainly, like all of our spiritual needs, our need for gratitude can be used against us. Recall when someone said to you, "You should be grateful." Were you angry? Did you feel judged? Gratitude is not meant to be "a should." When someone says, "You should be grateful," they often mean, "Stop complaining." Stop complaining, for example, about social and economic inequality. This is a ploy to keep us in our place, to maintain the established social order, whether that order is a family system, a national system, or a corporate system. Telling us we should feel gratitude will make us mad and squash any feelings of gratitude. Gratitude should not be a ploy of injustice.

Neither should gratitude lead to resignation, to becoming complacent about our lot in life. We can be grateful and still work hard to improve our life, maybe even harder than if we were not grateful. Gratitude can be empowering.

Gratitude does lead to generosity. When we fully embrace gratitude as an attitude, as a way of life, we want all of God's children to have what they need to survive and thrive. Gratitude and generosity go hand in hand. Wanting to give back is born in gratitude.

Generosity is not related to how rich or poor one is, but it does seem that when we are without, however we define "without," we appreciate all the more what we do have. And when we are fortunate, blessed, or favored once again, it is easier to feel grateful because we remember what it was like to be without. Some of the poorest people are also the most generous. But an attitude of gratitude is not based entirely on our earthly circumstances; it is also based on a spiritual perspective that can transcend human realities.

The research is now clear that gratitude is good for our mental health, social harmony, and even our physical health. Many self-help gurus promote various gratitude exercises as good for our mental health. I always find it amusing when modern science "discovers" a truth that most religious traditions have been telling us about for centuries. Indeed, gratitude is good for our mental health—no question about that! But gratitude, especially gratitude as an attitude, is also good for our spiritual health.

Analytical psychology suggests that we all have a collective unconscious—a part of our psyches that we have inherited from the generations before us, stretching all the way to prehistoric times. The content of our collective unconscious consists largely of universal symbols, images, myths, and archetypes. One of the memories we all have in the deepest recesses of our collective unconscious, dating back to when our ancestors were mostly hunter-gatherers, is that we are creatures; we are not the Creator. The appropriate spiritual response to this stirring in our soul is gratitude.

Reflection Questions and Activities

1. What do you do to help keep yourself conscious of being grateful?
2. Native American spirituality often has a humble, more grateful attitude toward the natural order than Western spirituality. Read a book that describes the spirituality of Native Americans.
3. Go on an occasional fast and then appreciate a delicious meal. "Fast food" can mean eating quickly and eating simply to consume. Learn about the Slow Food movement and take the time to appreciate and be grateful for your food.
4. Read the poem "Welcome Morning" by Ann Sexton. Meditate on it. In fact, try reading it each morning for a week.
5. What can you do to reduce the amount of things you have? Simplicity is a spiritual virtue in most religious traditions. When we have fewer possessions, we better appreciate what we have. Ascetic religious traditions are based on the idea that doing with less or doing without helps foster gratitude, trust, and humility. Interview a Catholic sister or brother, a Mennonite, or someone from a similar ascetic religious tradition who practices simplicity and ask them about their simple lifestyle.

13

Deliverance

Finding Real Deliverance from Our Slaveries

HUMANS ARE EASILY TRAPPED in all kinds of ways and to various degrees. This chapter focuses on two of the most widespread and crippling traps. First, many of us are trapped by our cravings and compulsions—our addictions. Others of us are trapped economically, politically, and socially. The reality of these entrapments and others like them is part of the human condition. It is in the nature of these entrapments to mold us into victims who feel powerless and helpless. We long to be free, but we cannot free ourselves. So, we look for a deliverer. This is the context of our spiritual need for deliverance.

In the affluent nations of the West, addiction is epidemic.

- Millions acknowledge being alcoholic, while millions more struggle with drinking problems.
- Millions struggle with their addiction to painkillers, illegal drugs, cigarettes, or pills.
- Millions struggle to manage their weight and overconsume food, especially sugar and processed foods.
- Thousands have a problem with gambling, and thousands more with pornography and sexual addiction.
- Some are addicted to anger, violence, and hate, with life-threatening consequences for all.

- Millions, especially our children, are hooked on their digital devices—to their games and social media.
- Some are obsessed with their body image.
- Some are obsessed with money, power, and the accumulation of wealth.

Should I go on?

Addiction takes many forms in modern societies, is widespread, and is reinforced and encouraged by our capitalistic culture and its primary instrument of entrapment: aggressive, multimedia advertising campaigns. We all struggle with our "preferred" addiction.

For some of us, quite frankly, the demons have won;

for others, we can manage our cravings; and

for still others, our compulsions have transformed into relatively positive outlets.

The degree of our entrapment certainly varies from person to person. Yet, one way or another, we are all paying a high price in terms of our personal health, mental health, family relationships, and the moral fabric of our nation. It's ironic, isn't it, that among Americans, who proclaim their freedom and prize their independence, so many of us have so little psychological freedom or true independence.

When the consequences of our addiction catch up with us, we try various avenues to escape the addiction.

- We try psychotherapy.
- We try religion.
- We try various medical "fixes," including pharmacological interventions.
- We try self-help programs.
- We enroll in addiction treatment programs of one form or another.

The most widespread program that addresses the problem of addiction, especially alcohol and drug addiction, is the 12-step program. The 12-step model is, in its own words, essentially a spiritual program; it is a spiritual answer or alternative to addiction. It is based on a set of widely acknowledged spiritual principles. These principles include

surrendering to one's Higher Power	mutual respect
mutual accountability	inclusivity
community support	nonjudgmental attitude
empowerment	humanistic values
doing the inner hard work	ethical norms
forgiveness	absolute anonymity
democratic program structure	personal honesty and vulnerability

A 12-step program is not the answer for everyone or for every form of addiction, but it is the most successful pathway to recovery. Yes, there are other medical and psychosocial interventions that are effective, particularly with some types of addiction, whether used alone or in concert with a 12-step program. But unless the problem is addressed on a spiritual level, or at least a holistic level, the prescribed intervention only puts a temporary fix over the wound, fixes one addiction with another, or allows the suppressed cravings to resurface later. You might say that a 12-step program does not provide a savior but is a process that, if worked, promises deliverance.

But let's change focus for a minute. People can be entrapped by social, economic, or political oppression. This form of entrapment also comes in various forms and degrees. Humans have been enslaving other humans almost from the dawn of time. There is still physical slavery in the world, such as the enslavement of young women and children in the sex trade. Physical slavery is made possible by violence, power, and drug abuse, all of which suggest a heinous connection between the slavery to addiction and the slavery of other human beings. It does seem to some who are in the throes of addiction that there is a demonic power at work in the world that is bent on attacking human freedom and independence.

Economic entrapment is more subtle, comprehensive, and indirect. In America, one of the richest nations in the world, poverty shows up in the form of homelessness and is found in situational poverty, the working poor, food insecurity, income inequity, and the need to work multiple jobs. Most people in these circumstances feel trapped by their economic situation. People of color and marginalized people feel especially trapped, not just by economic structures but also by the dynamics of discrimination and racism.

Political entrapment takes the obvious form of dictatorships or theocracies, which control their populaces with regulations, punishments, and disinformation. Religion is not immune to this evil. Some religious cults, or religious leaders who are often themselves addicts, enslave their followers through false promises, brainwashing, and threats of eternal punishment. Such religious activities are, to my mind, a form of religious abuse.

People who are trapped economically, socially, and politically feel powerless. Like people struggling with chemical and behavioral additions, oppressed people often feel helpless. Helplessness, along with denial, are the tools that reinforce oppression and addiction.

Helplessness is learned.

Helplessness is self-reinforcing.

Helplessness is the hallmark of a victim mentality.

Out of this helplessness or victim mentality, we look for a savior—a political leader, a military leader, or a religious leader who will rise up and lead us to the promised land. Often, this rebellion is accomplished by violence. Perhaps we come to believe through a campaign of disinformation that we are free, or will be free in time, once the overlords are killed. Violence in one form or another has always been the tool of the slave masters and the false deliverers. And often, these false deliverers do more damage than good, creating a society that is new in name only. We, the people, are still oppressed, but now in a new or perhaps a more subtle way.

We do not need any more cartoon superheroes. There are no superheroes. Anyone who promises that they alone can fix all our problems is selling us snake oil. We need to fix our own problems through hard work, community building, empowerment, and mutual accountability. These are the principles that make a 12-step program work. These same principles will work to liberate a people or a nation as well.

What we often fail to understand, as recovering people remind us, is that the problem is in us. The parallels between addiction and economic, social, or political entrapment are not exact, but one of the common dynamics is a victim mentality. The victim mentality makes us feel trapped, helpless, and hopeless. Because of this mentality, we inevitably want a savior, a deliverer, someone to rescue us. While this a genuine spiritual need, how we get this need fulfilled is critical. Some deliverers, even if they are well meaning, will only maintain the addictive system (our victimization). A life-giving or authentic solution is found in us when we are empowered. No one from the outside, especially a person promising a quick fix or violence as a means of deliverance, is going to save us. Until we do the inside work and deal with our desire to have a savior, we will not be liberated.

As a Chinese aphorism, rooted in Buddhist teaching, puts it, "If you meet the Buddha on the road, kill him." This phrase, while harsh, reminds us that anyone who promises to deliver us, even a religious figure, should be rejected.

Professionals who work with disadvantaged communities talk about empowerment and liberation. Poor people can free themselves from economic, social, and political oppression only by

- working together in community,
- working to educate themselves,
- working and empowering one another,
- questioning the disinformation and propaganda of the oppressors or oppressing corporations, and
- forming deep roots in a spiritual perspective and reality.

In other words, deliverance takes work.

Becoming truly free from addiction or from other forms of entrapment requires work. There is no savior who will do the work for us. We must liberate ourselves using spiritual principles. In the case of addiction, we must do the hard work of a 12-step program and maintain a sober lifestyle. In the case of political or social oppression, we must do the work of organizing ourselves and living into a new style of community empowerment and political engagement. A nation's salvation does not lie in one person, one savior, however charismatic they may be, but in the process of democratic engagement.

An important tool in the work to overcome our entrapment, whether we are caught in an internal or external prison, is knowledge. Today's slave masters have public relations departments! The peddlers of alcohol, drugs, fast food, sexual pleasure, and easy money are everywhere on television and social media, denying or minimizing the dangers of their products and activities. The political and economic slave masters have propaganda, too. Individuals and corporations are making tons of money by keeping us thinking like consumers; keeping us in debt; keeping us believing, however naively, in the American dream; keeping us uninformed, deceived by the false promises of salvation; and keeping us poor so that there is more for them.

Knowledge is the first step; education is invaluable.

Community is the second step, working together for the common good.

Spirituality is the third step, a spirituality dependent not on a savior but on our own empowerment.

My point is that even though our need for deliverance is a spiritual need, the solution lies not in a savior but in a process—the process of empowerment, hard work, and community building that makes liberation possible. There is no savior, but there is a saving pathway. Interestingly, the earliest Christians referred to their faith as the Way, a way of life, a process of renewal, which Christian mystics would later call the way of the cross. The way of the Buddha is the path to enlightenment and liberation from suffering. The truly helpful religions of the world offer not a savior but a spiritual path. That pathway requires work and surrender, critical thinking, community building, accountability, and inner work, but it is the way to deliverance for those of us who suffer under the yoke of any kind of slavery.

Reflection Questions and Activities

1. What is the addiction you struggle with the most? What has worked and not worked to help you manage your entrapment? Rate how severe or destructive your addictive behavior is in your life and your relationships.
2. Find an Open AA meeting near you and attend it. You do not have to share if you do not want to. Just listen. There is a lot to learn by listening.
3. What spiritual practices help you calm your cravings, obsessions, or compulsions for your addictive substance or activity?
4. View a dramatic production of *Waiting for Godot* by Samuel Beckett, which is one of the most significant plays of the twentieth century. What themes do you see in the play that highlight, concur with, or offer a different viewpoint on our spiritual need for deliverance?
5. What do you think of the idea that chemical and behavioral addictions are connected to political, social, and economic oppressions? How are they similar, and how are they different?

14

Connections

Staying Connected with Deceased Loved Ones

We humans have deep emotional attachments to our families. Admittedly, these attachments can be complicated and ambiguous, but they are always important. They are also necessary for our physical, mental, and emotional health. In the same breath, we must acknowledge that we lose those we love—inevitably and universally—by various means, but ultimately by death. This is the nature of the human condition: attachment and loss. So, sooner or later we stand by the graveside of a loved one and our heart aches with sorrow. In these moments, we have a spiritual need to believe in something that will enable us to stay connected, to ease our pain.

In most cultures, this need is met by the belief in an afterlife, the conviction that our deceased loved ones are still accessible to us, and, in many cases, that we will be together again in heaven or that family relationships transcend death.

Family bonds vary in many ways. Some are quite strong, others not so much. Some are endearing, others not so much. Some are healthy, others more toxic. Indeed, most family relations have a mixture of healthy and unhealthy elements. Most are a mixture of love and anger, enmeshment and individuation, security and independence.

Most of us, however, have one or several significant family relationships whose loss would be overwhelming, especially if our loved one dies tragically, unexpectedly, or cruelly. Our pain would be overwhelming. It would compel us to stay connected in any way possible. Yes, we have our memories, photographs, stories, family histories, and favorite music. These are all ways to stay close to our loved ones, to find comfort in our sorrow.

But the thought that there is nothing after death is almost intolerable. How can this love we experienced just vanish? How can everything that is unique and priceless about this person just dissolve into ashes? Something within us rises up: "No, there must be something more! They must be alive, in some form or another." We want our deceased loved ones to be accessible to us.

Most religious traditions around the globe have responded to this spiritual need by positing an afterlife, which people in the Western religious traditions call heaven. The character of heaven varies from religion to religion. Some versions have entrance requirements; others do not. For most religious traditions, heaven is an alternative universe, a reality where the deceased exists, lives on, or will live again. Heaven is always a nonphysical reality, not locatable on a map, but everyone there maintains their physical identity. In addition, heaven is

- a place of peace, where suffering has ceased;
- a place of love and harmony;
- a place of justice, where the rights and wrongs of this life have been set right;
- a place of transformation, where the souls who are there are better versions of their earthly selves: and
- most of all, it is a place where we will meet our loved ones again.

Heaven is a very comforting vision for those of us in mourning.

Of all of life's losses, the death of one's child is the most heartbreaking. Early in my career, I had the privilege of walking alongside two young parents who had to bury their six-year-old daughter, the victim of a random act of violence. As fate would have it, they were at the same time expecting their second child in a few months. They wanted to grieve "hard and fast" (if that is possible) so they would be emotionally ready to welcome their new baby. Fortunately, they had many friends and a flexible mortician who allowed them all to get their hands dirty as they buried Sally in a little wooden casket, one trowel of dirt at a time. It was one of the most powerful grief rituals I have ever participated in.

In my humble message to the grieving parents, I invited them to close their eyes and envision Sally alive, smiling, wearing her favorite dress, and even giggling as she ran through a sunny meadow on a spring day and soared on a tree swing, which she loved to do in her earthly life. The gathered community embraced this vision for a while. It was so comforting; tears flowed, and it was hard not to imagine that somewhere, somehow, this vision was real.

After a few minutes, I added, "Now imagine Sally growing up . . . yes, making new friends . . . going to summer camp . . . attending high school . . . even becoming a mother herself someday." This was a more difficult vision, but I was convinced that in the heaven I trusted in, Sally would get a chance to grow up and live the life she was robbed of in this world.

Another common feature of these afterlives or heavens is that this alternative reality interfaces with our daily reality. The departed can communicate with us and we with them, although not in ordinary ways. They can send us messages, offer guidance or a pearl of wisdom, or, in rare cases, intervene in this world. The most common message from a departed loved one is a message of peace and well-being, such as "I'm okay" or "It is well." On other occasions, the message from beyond, or even a visit from beyond, takes the form of an instruction or encouragement: "You can do this!" or "I am with you."

Many religions also believe that we who are living can influence and shape the well-being of the departed through our prayers, indulgences, good deeds, ritual acts, and honoring of them on significant anniversaries. The messages we want to communicate to the departed often are "We will be okay" or "We miss you."

The doors between this reality and the afterlife are not controllable or predictable and are subject to much abuse, but the doors exist and occasionally swing open in mysterious ways. This is another common feature of the reality of the afterlife.

All of this leads to the observation that when someone we love dearly dies, it is not always true that the person is completely lost to us. It is more like our relationship with them has not ended, just changed. Instead of a flesh-and-blood relationship, we now have a spiritual relationship, a spiritual connection.

The loved ones of many people around the world continue to be sources of guidance, comfort, and strength for those mourning their death. For some, these ancestors are not just the most recently lost loved ones but also their ancestors of earlier generations. The collective wisdom of our ancestors can be a great source of wisdom and spiritual guidance. Some religions broaden the scope of this "cloud of witnesses" to include saints, those who are our spiritual ancestors if not our biological ancestors.

This impulse to stay connected can easily drift into the practice of ancestral worship, that is, to giving our deceased ancestors magical powers. People inclined to worship their ancestors or their chosen saint do so by creating shrines and performing rituals designed to maintain the good favor of the deceased or inviting them to become present to help them in their time of need or guide them with the wisdom of the ages.

Ancestor worship is often closely tied to ethnic identity and family bonds and reinforces these connections, which can be a good thing. This does help keep families connected. It can also be used to compel us to participate in various ethnic or family-based political or social causes. A young person might be told, for example, that they need to join a war effort: "By risking your life for your nation, you are doing what your great-grandfather did, and he would be proud of you." More benignly, a young person might be told, "Your grandmother wants you to be a veterinarian like your mother and her mother before her." Or, "This farm has been in our family for generations. How can you consider selling it?" A healthy appreciation of the legacy of one's loved ones must be balanced with freedom of choice and a recognition of the uniqueness of the present time.

You may remember with a smile the scene from the movie *Fiddler on the Roof* in which Tevye explains to his wife, Golde, why he is changing his mind and allowing their eldest daughter to marry the tailor instead of the previously arranged marriage to the older village butcher. He says he had a dream or vision in which their ancestors warned of the union with the butcher and threatened to curse it if it proceeded. This startling message from beyond the grave alarms Golde, and she insists that he must allow their daughter to marry her heart's desire. In a conversation with the Almighty, Tevye gives a wry smile, winks, and sings the theme song, "Tradition."

Warmly and humorously, this episode illustrates the power, craziness, and potential abuse that can come with too much reliance on one's ancestors. On the one hand, the presence of our ancestors is a great source of comfort in times of loss and even a support in times of trial. On the other hand, we are prone to project our unfinished issues, conflicts, and agendas onto blank heavenly screens.

- Do our departed loved ones empower us or entrap us?

- Can our vision of an afterlife comfort us without blocking our grief?
- Can the belief in an eternal paradise motivate some people to take their own life, perhaps as a noble sacrifice?
- Do we want to hear from our dead loved one so much that we will believe anything a psychic tells us?
- Does heaven or an afterlife reinforce our denial of death?

In short, what kind of afterlife offers us a life-affirming way to get our spiritual need for connections fulfilled?

I like to think that people change when they die and go to heaven, that in their heavenly state they are transformed into nicer people—

people who want the best for us,

people who are wise now in ways they were not in this life,

people who truly love us and want what is best for us.

If our messages from beyond are not in this spirit, then we must question whether our own continuing toxic views are clouding what we are hearing.

All of this points to a more general but important lesson in life: how to learn from the past but not be trapped by the past. How do we learn from those who have gone before us but not be fixated on them or limited by their values or perceived views? The future is ever unfolding, and life is found in going forward.

Reflection Questions and Activities

1. Thinking about your deceased loved ones, who do you long to stay connected to the most? Why? Write a letter to this person.
2. Paint or draw your vision of the afterlife.
3. Does believing in the reality of the afterlife make it easier or harder to grieve the loss of a loved one? In what ways?
4. Have you ever received a message from beyond, from a deceased loved one? How did you evaluate its authenticity? Was the message helpful and life-giving, or was it toxic in some way?
5. Find the poem "Love Letter from the Afterlife" by Andrea Gibson. Read it several times and reflect on the spiritual need to connect.

15

Forgiveness

Accepting Our Fallibility through Grace

We humans are fallible. We inevitably make mistakes. No one is perfect; everyone makes mistakes. This is our reality—another aspect of the human condition.

- Some of the mistakes we make are accidents. We feel bad about these mistakes; we apologize and try to make amends.
- Some of the mistakes we make are due to inadequate or faulty information. Our intentions were honorable—we just did not have enough information. We say, "If only I knew then what I know now."
- In other cases, we made mistakes because we were ill or were enslaved by addictive forces.
- In still other cases, we knew full well what the right course of action should have been, but we lacked the moral courage to take it.

In any event, we have made mistakes. And they will probably not be the last mistakes we make, either. If one thing is certain in life—besides death and taxes—it is that we will make mistakes.

All this is not to say that we humans do not learn from our mistakes. We do. Our mistakes have led to progress in various human endeavors. One of the lessons we have learned is that humans are fallible. So, we have put into place quality assurance programs, a government with checks and balances, and even such things as morality police—all designed to reduce the incidence of mistakes. And yet, we still make mistakes. We have hurt others and have been hurt. On some occasions, people have even died because of our mistakes, directly or indirectly. We have all been wronged by or harmed another person.

Forgiveness is a need that is often facilitated fairly successfully on the human plane in the contexts of family reunions, a therapist's office, or more formally through the justice system. Most of the time, at the end of such proceedings, we feel forgiven or we have extended forgiveness. But this is not always the case.

- What happens when the person we wronged is now deceased or does not wish to have any contact with us? How do we secure or give forgiveness then?
- Can we forgive even if the offender does not acknowledge any wrongdoing?
- How is forgiveness secured when another person's or our own sin is so grievous, so heinous or massive, even if done by accident, that no amount of pardon is adequate?
- Are some acts—genocide, child abuse, sexual slavery, massacres—by their very nature unforgivable?
- Is there forgiveness for what we did not do but wanted to do?
- What if our sin was against future generations or planet Earth? Who forgives us then?
- What if we keep repeating the same sin over and over? On the human plane, won't our apologies now fall on deaf ears? Is there any forgiveness for us?

In cases such as these, forgiveness must involve a spiritual dimension, a dynamic beyond the human plane. Forgiveness is not possible in these circumstances without a connection to a loving, forgiving Divine Reality.

My client James was raised by his single mother and remained close to her all her life. Yet when she was suffering through the latter stages of cancer, his business and his wife prevented him from visiting her as much as he would have liked. When she died, he was not there at her bedside, and he later heard from her nurses that his mother, in a delusional state, called out for him. These tales haunted James for years. He sought someone's forgiveness—his mother's, his own, maybe God's. All our work in counseling only moved the needle a little, and the sermons of James's pastor moved it only a little more. Resolution came unexpectedly years later when an unusual butterfly fluttered over his head as if to say hello, which he interpreted as a message from his mother. The message was, "I am at peace. All is forgiven." This was a simple, perhaps even trivial event in the grand scheme of things, but James needed something from beyond the human plane—a word of grace, I might call it.

Not everyone has access to a fair, corruption-free judicial system. Not every legal ruling is satisfying to those seeking to be forgiven or to forgive. Some crimes are so cruel, so horrific, so inhumane that no measure of this world's justice seems adequate. In such circumstances, forgiveness and even justice become a spiritual need. Thus, many have turned to the domain of religion to find true justice and forgiveness. In the monotheistic religions, for example, God is understood as the ultimate judge. In the world to come, all wrongs will be made right. All tears will be wiped away because there will be justice and mercy.

Forgiveness is interwoven with justice.

Forgiveness is easier after justice is served.

Forgiveness is hard when there is no justice.

On this side of heaven, humans have turned to religion to secure forgiveness and justice, both in contemporary cultures and in earlier times. Each world religion or denomination has various rites, practices, and procedures that its adherents can use to facilitate forgiveness. For example, to secure forgiveness, people go to confession, make sacrifices, and perform acts of repentance and restitution. Some people engage in a discipline of cleansing or purifying themselves so that they are both forgiven and protected against committing the same sin again. If people fail to repent or confess, then each religion also outlines consequences of their omissions. Some of these consequences are in this life, some in the next life. The various religious ways of facilitating forgiveness sometimes work. Many people become able to do what they could not do on their own: forgive the unforgivable. Others seem only to cycle through the rites without any lasting peace.

Forgiveness, of course, assumes that there is some standard, expectation, or law that one has violated. Forgiveness assumes an authority, whether it is a divine authority, civil authority, or our own internal standard. Religions without a clear concept of sin or a monotheistic God may not speak of forgiveness in quite the same way as Western religions but have parallel concepts. Every religion has some way of helping its adherents deal with their own fallibility because ultimately coming to terms with one's mistakes is a universal spiritual need.

To err is human, to forgive divine. It is not easy for us humans to forgive. Sometimes we need divine help. Forgiveness requires that we embrace the pain—the pain of our mistake, the hurt caused by another's actions, and the painful acknowledgment of our own fallibility.

It is easy to deny or bury our pain. Forgiveness can be hard and painful work. It is tempting to run from forgiveness-to deny, delay or avoid it—sometimes until it is too late. There is a wise adage that, when ending a relationship, there are three important things to say: "I love you," "Thank you," and "I forgive you; please forgive me." We might be too busy or too upset to say these words, but without these conversations, it is difficult to move on.

I had occasion to talk with James again a year or so after his epiphany with the butterfly. He had drifted back into despair and shame over how he had handled his relationship to his mother's dying. He acknowledged that the butterfly experience was a gift and that he no longer felt that his mother was angry with him, but, he reflected, he was still disappointed in himself. He said,

"I expected more of myself."

"I should have handled it all so differently."

"It could have been a wonderful moment for Mom and me."

Even when we access the spiritual realm or a spiritual perspective to secure or give forgiveness, we may fail to realize forgiveness because we sabotage our own efforts and thereby deny ourselves the full benefits of forgiveness.

So, let's turn our attention to the issue of self-forgiveness, not just in terms of individual acts but in terms of our inability to forgive ourselves for being imperfect or, in other words, fallible. The common manifestation of this inability is perfectionism in its many variations. Perfectionism is a brutal and heinous psychological dynamic, almost an epidemic in modern culture. Its sinister components include self-hate, self-criticism, overcompensating through egoism and narcissism, denial of reality, and obsessive fault-finding. Perfectionism is very painful, and many people drown that pain in alcohol or struggle with depression.

For those of us who tend to be perfectionists, self-forgiveness is very hard. It is easier for us to forgive someone else than to forgive ourselves.

We find it hard to admit that we all make mistakes.

We think we are special and don't make mistakes.

We find it hard to forgive ourselves, to embrace our fallibility.

It is true—we can be our own worst critic!

Some vocations actually attract or create perfectionists. Medical professionals, airline pilots, accountants, certain kinds of artists, and religious people all come to mind. People in the public eye, even in this immoral age, go to great lengths to hide their failures, to deny any wrongdoing, rather than openly and honestly admitting their mistakes and asking for forgiveness. Why is asking for forgiveness so hard in our civil life? Is it that we see being forgiven as a weakness?

To really, truly forgive ourselves, not just once but as a state of being, is to accept our fallibility. For this kind of forgiveness, we need to reach beyond the human plane to the spiritual plane. We need some higher authority to tell us we are forgiven, that we are accepted and are good even though we have failed. We need a power to release us from our self-condemnation. Only by accepting our fallible nature can we learn from our mistakes and move on.

In many religions or spiritual traditions, this deeper spiritual need to accept our fallibility is communicated through the concept of grace. Grace is always a word from beyond us, telling us that

we are accepted,

our mistakes are a gift, and

we can learn from our mistakes.

Our mistakes are the means by which we learn and grow. It is about progress, not perfection, as my AA friends say.

If we embrace grace, letting it wash over us and cleanse us of our self-recrimination, we can more easily forgive both others and ourselves. Grace leads to self-acceptance, the cornerstone of a healthy personality.

Most spiritual traditions have a similar or related concept of grace. More importantly, they have prescribed pathways to realize this ultimate forgiveness.

- The path is both easy and not easy.
- It is long and not over in a day.

- It is something we do alone and in community.
- It requires hard work and is something we receive as a gift.
- It is a gift of love from the Divine.

Ultimately, grace must come not just from human lips or the jury box but from our spiritual connection to a higher authority, a benevolent spiritual parent that can help us accept our inherent fallibility.

Reflection Questions and Activities

1. How strong is your need for forgiveness? Does your fallibility bother you deeply?
2. Martin Doblmeier's 2008 documentary *The Power of Forgiveness* is available online or as a DVD. As you view this film, notice how religion and spirituality are interwoven with the ability or inability to forgive.
3. Is forgiveness for the one being forgiven or is it for the one doing the forgiving?
4. A wise person once said, "Nothing is wasted in the spiritual journey." Reflect on this phrase and write about what it means to you.
5. The root meaning of the verb "to forgive" is "to give up" or "to give away." What are we giving up if we forgive someone who has wronged us?

16

Transformation

Seeking Pathways to New Life or Rebirth

Life is not what it is supposed to be. We humans are not what we are supposed to be. There is something wrong with all of us. We keep screwing up! We try to do wonderful things, and sometimes we succeed, but we sense that there is something wrong with us, collectively and individually. As we become aware of this wrongness, we recognize our spiritual need for transformation or rebirth.

Humans have made great progress technologically and materially over the centuries, but it could also be argued that we have not made parallel progress morally. We still are controlled by the impulses, instincts, and desires of our prehistoric selves, or what some neurologists call our reptilian brains. We are still largely immature, violent, and selfish children, but now our toys are nuclear weapons! If we wish to avoid self-destruction, we humans need to find ways to morph into a better version of ourselves.

On the personal level, too, many of us are not content with our lives. Our discontent may take various forms and expressions. We might be discontented with our economic condition. We might be unhappy with our physical health, appearance, or gender. We might be unhappy with our personal relationships, our work, or our nation. We want to change. We want to be happier, to be better people, to be healthier in mind, body, and spirit.

Such discontent, such longing for change, is certainly common and widespread. Who among us has not longed to redo our life, to be born again but knowing what we know now, of course. "Now that I know what

I know. . ." We humans engage in various activities in an effort to change. We attend classes, read self-help books, enroll in workshops on personal effectiveness or adjustment, look for new jobs, relocate to a different community or state, and even change our appearance. Sometimes this works, but sometimes it does not.

What happens when these types of changes or paths to change are not effective? We may then come to embrace the words of Pogo: "We have met the enemy, and he is us." For some, this realization comes as a crisis, a reckoning, or a "hitting bottom." Changing various external factors is not enough. Moving the deck chairs on the *Titanic* is not enough. We must change ourselves on a deeper level, at the level of our heart, soul, attitude, and/or character. Religious people call this rebirth—a do-over of our life.

In this modern age, psychotherapy has become an acceptable and common activity through which people seek to change themselves. Psychotherapy, the secular form of spiritual transformation, offers us rebirth through a careful exploration of our past, inner life, emotions, and/or faulty thinking. Such exploration leads to change, hopefully in the direction of our "better angels" but not necessarily.

One of the chief principles of psychotherapy is that the client must really want to change if psychotherapy is to be successful, in part because change is hard work. At its best, therapy does offer us the opportunity to change ourselves, with the supportive guidance of a therapist. However, not everyone has access to therapeutic services. Plus, therapy works for some people but not for others. Sometimes it works for a time or in partial ways. We may long for something more.

Thus, some of us ultimately come, hat in hand, to the door of religion, seeking a still deeper change, a change that I call a transformation—a spiritual transformation. Those of us who come to religion may do so because we are desperate, because our pain is great, or because other efforts to change have failed.

- We long to be healed from a hurt.
- We long to be free from an addiction.
- We long to be reconciled.
- We long to be made whole.

Yet, in a sense, we all experience elements of this need, this deep longing, to transform ourselves and to be different, better, freer, and healthier.

Dennis came to my counseling office, unannounced and without an appointment but excited and agitated. I made some time for him. He wanted to tell me that Jesus Christ had entered his heart and wiped away his sins, and he was "born again." He had been attending a program in town called Victory Outreach, offered by a Christian evangelical church that specialized in ministering to ex-cons and drug addicts—people not usually found in mainline congregations. Dennis's enthusiasm was contagious. I enjoyed our talks. He would come back to see me occasionally when he could not get "the demons out of his head," which was his way of talking about his cravings. I think I learned more from Dennis than he did from me. It was insightful that he framed his struggle as spiritual warfare. I did not always understand or resonate with his language and imagery, but I understood his struggle. It is the process we all enter into—those of us who long for a new life and those who struggle to maintain our new life.

If we examine the ways of faith around the world, is it not true that every religion, in one way or another, offers transformation or rebirth? Religion is about change, about conversion, and about life-changing experiences. Most of the time, the promised transformation process is life-long, not short and dramatic. Most of the time, transformation comes about through faithful practice of the religion's rites and disciplines.

Does not every religion promise a spiritual rebirth? Is that not one of the basic human spiritual needs that religion traditionally seeks to meet?

Each religion, of course, defines for itself what the nature of the "wrongness" is, what the true problem of humanity or human existence is. Each religion then explains why other solutions have not worked. Next, each religion offers its adherents a vision of what its followers can become, should they be transformed. Finally, each religion offers processes by which believers can sustain the transformation after it has occurred or, if the transformation is a gradual process, can sustain the process of transformation.

Christianity, for example, says that the problem is sin and that through faith in Jesus Christ one can be transformed and experience more "fruits of faith." Islam says that the ultimate problem is idolatry and that through faithful obedience to the four pillars of Islam, one can find contentment for one's soul. Buddhism says that humanity's basic problem is rooted in our attachments and suffering (summarized in the Four Noble Truths) and that by practicing the path of Buddha, we can find inner contentment through reducing ours desires and thus our suffering. In many ways, transformation is the essence of religion. Religion at its core tries to redo human nature one way or another.

Some religions offer the world various kinds of collective transformation as well, arguing that collective transformation is a more effective way to change human nature than an individualistic approach. Throughout the centuries, religious groups have attempted to transform society or culture according to their moral or religious principles. Some religious groups have separated themselves from the dominant culture, physically isolating themselves in order to create an ideal community, a utopia. Often such experiments are characterized by individual purification programs coupled with the offer of a new support community or family. Other religious groups work to transform an existing nation-state in ways designed to create an ideal "new" society, a theocracy. Unfortunately, both of these approaches have downsides. The suppression of human creativity, freedom, and basic rights are some of the common negatives. There is something about striving to be better morally, either individually or collectively, that makes us think we are better than others, those we call gentiles, pagans, or infidels. All too often, such divisiveness leads to conflict. Human nature is hard to transform, is it not?

Transformation is the litmus test of a religion's authenticity.

- Nothing is more powerful than a believer whose life has been transformed.
- Nothing speaks more to a religion's truth than such "results."
- Nothing attracts believers to a new church, temple, or even cult more than the excitement that surrounds new life.

Certainly, not all transformations are dramatic, sudden, and spectacular. Some of the best and most lasting transformations occur gradually and quietly over a long period of time. But what happens to a church, denomination, or religion that has lost its transformative power? It fades away . . . and then new forms of religious life arise that address our spiritual need for transformation!

What has been said about organized religion can be applied equally to quasi-religious movements, such as social and political causes. These movements also have worldviews that describe a wrongness—with the current state of affairs, with us humans, with the nation, or with the world in general. These movements also offer a prescription to solve the problem, or a vision of the ideal world, and describe how to get there. But we should ask questions, examine the evidence, and consider alternative pathways before we hop on the bandwagon.

Perhaps, too, we should examine carefully the ultimate goal of a religion or any transformative process before entering into that process. Who are the saints of this religion? Who are the heroes of this cause? Do we want to turn out like them?

Next, we must realize that authentic transformation is a process, not a dramatic event. It takes work and practice—a sustained effort. Anyone who promises us an instant new life or a miraculous rebirth must be questioned.

- We are looking for a process, not a religion.
- We are looking for a process that is fundamentally and authentically spiritual.
- We are looking for a process that is focused on progress, not perfection.
- We are looking for a process that blends discipline and acceptance.
- We are looking for a process that offers us fellow travelers, both human and divine.

Perhaps not all transformations are equally morally valid. The great religions of the world agree in general on basic moral values, but there are many variations on the rule, even within each religion, not to mention in the realm of personality cults, pseudo-religions, and social or political movements of one kind or another. Our hunger for transformation is so great, especially for some of us, that we jump into almost anything that promises new life. Instead, we must be good consumers in the spiritual marketplace. We must temper our need for transformation with discernment and wisdom. We must feed our spiritual need with healthy food and not be fooled by the false promises of junk food.

The Christian Scriptures encourage people to engage in this process of transformation and "work out your own salvation with fear and trembling" (Philippians 2:12). Yes, indeed! The process of transformation is a journey, a discovery, a work in process, and it offers the pearl of great price: new life.

Reflection Questions and Activities

1. What would you say is wrong with humans or with human existence? How does your religious tradition, if any, address this wrongness?
2. Do you personally long for change? For rebirth? What have you tried to change? How has that worked out for you?

3. Do you think that people can truly transform individually, or must we do it as a community, mutually supporting one another toward a common goal?
4. Identify a poem that is about transformation, personal or collective. Can daily poetry reading or memorizing be an effective tool for personal transformation?
5. View the movie *Good Will Hunting* (1997), which is about personal transformation. What elements of transformation are portrayed in this film?

17

Courage

Finding Courage beyond Our Human Resources

Life is filled with crises that test us. Some of these crises are life-threatening. Some involve ambiguous moral choices, such as between two relatively bad choices. Some are public; others are private. All have significant, sometimes overwhelming consequences. In the face of such crises, where do we get the courage to act? Most of us do have some resources we can draw upon, but what if the courage that is required is beyond us? In such circumstances, courage becomes a spiritual need.

- Soldiers, public safety officers and first responders face such situations quite regularly. They have to be brave. They have to run up a burning staircase, or jump out of an airplane, or rescue people unable to help themselves.
- Explorers, such as astronauts, need courage to launch themselves in a rocket into the unknown, into an airless, cold, and merciless environment. They do it for science, for humankind, maybe even for fame.
- Journalists need courage from time to time—the courage to investigate a story that is not popular or to secure information controlled or suppressed by the powerful. Journalists risk life and limb daily to bring us the impartial information we need.
- The prophets among us know the courage required to "speak truth to power." Speaking up, speaking out, and standing up for one's convictions requires courage.

- Sometimes it takes courage to choose certain medical procedures. When we have a significant surgery, it takes courage to "go under," knowing we will endure pain, discomfort, and a long recovery and may not even wake up at all.
- Leaders at all levels of government and civic organizations need courage to choose to put the good of the people ahead of partisan politics or even their desire to be re-elected.
- Deciding in the face of ambiguity takes its own kind of courage. Sometimes we do not know what the right thing to do is, but the circumstances of the moment are urgent and we must choose, for better or worse—God help us! Making a decision can take courage.
- Sometimes it takes courage to risk being wrong.
- Sometimes it takes courage to restrain ourselves in the face of verbal insults.
- Some decisions in life are not so much about life and death as they are morally challenging. The cadets at West Point have a prayer that includes this petition: help us "choose the harder right instead of the easier wrong." It takes courage to choose the right action.
- For some of us, it takes courage just to do the ordinary things in life. People with disabilities need courage to put one foot in front of another. So do people in chronic pain, poor people looking for work, children standing up to bullies, or recovering people not using drugs or drinking alcohol.

In hundreds and thousands of ways, some huge and many more small, life requires courage of us. For some of the courageous among us, courage is a way of life, a pathway to God, and/or a style of living. For most of us, courage is a challenge, a test of character, and occasionally an existential choice.

What is courage? Courage is overcoming our fears, our natural and innate fears. Not all of us are able to easily set aside our fears. Courage may be more difficult for some of us than for others. Being brave is acting in spite of our fear. That is a good definition of courage: "acting in spite of fear."

Courage is not natural. As my grandmother used to say, "Courage is not for the faint of heart." It is natural to fear—to fear danger, to fear pain. Bravery is not very common, really. But people can be brave from time to time, when they see the greater good,

when the choice is clear and compelling, and

when they have support.

We admire such people. They are the best among us. They are our heroes. And sometimes our brave heroes lose their lives or become injured. In such circumstances, we honor their sacrifice.

To sacrifice oneself for another, even unto death, is not natural. Yes, most of us would sacrifice ourselves for a loved one, but would we do so for a stranger, for a principle, or for a nation? That is rare. It is not natural; it is sometimes even supernatural. Remember the passengers aboard Flight 93 on September 11, 2001. They realized that their plane had been hijacked by terrorists who were intending to crash it into Washington, DC. Imagine the courage it took for them to rise up, knowing they were probably going to die but that, if successful, they could prevent the deaths of thousands more. When I think of courage, I think of them.

We are accustomed to thinking of spirituality as a source of inner peace, serenity, and tranquility amid the storms of life. And in this modern world, where we experience so much stress and anxiety, many are increasingly turning to spirituality to help manage stress. In this regard, relaxation exercises and mindfulness meditation have become popular, even almost synonymous with spirituality. Perhaps spirituality can also be a source of energy, empowerment, and the courage to take bold action.

Situations that require great courage are often the impetus for spiritual conversion or personal renewal. Many soldiers, for example, find religion on the battlefield when they are required to be brave, brave beyond their human resources. Many people facing surgery, torture, imprisonment, or a life full of risk are forced to connect to their Higher Power. The connection between courage and spirituality is deep because it sometimes takes spiritual empowerment to do courageous things.

Religion tends to "encourage" us to be our better selves and to sacrifice when necessary for the greater good. Faith and courage overlap a bit, right? Actually, courage is a kind of faith, a leap of faith. But courage is more than trust—courage requires action, a decision, putting our life on the line. Courage is faith demonstrated in action.

Another interesting word is "inspiration." We often need inspiration to be courageous. Inspiration is the fuel for courage. Inspiration makes courageous acts possible. Both of these words, encourage ("to give courage") and inspiration ("infused with spirit"), suggest the interweaving of courage and spirituality. Where do we find inspiration?

Religion's connection with courage has a dark side, however. Courage seems like a morally good thing, and most often it is, but it does not have to be. Terrorists give up their lives for their mission objective, and that requires courage. From the perspective of the victims of their terror, the terrorists are acting out of blind obedience or delusions of grandeur, but from the perspective of the individual terrorist, they are showing great bravery. We may make a courageous decision that to our mind is the right thing to do, but it may actually be ill informed or lack a wider perspective. We need to remind ourselves to think critically, have an ethical perspective, and gather as much information as possible, if time permits. And courage needs to be balanced with love.

What helps us have courage in risky moments? We can draw courage from many ordinary human sources:

from friends,

from family,

from heroes,

from our faith,

from our convictions regarding what is right, and

from good information.

Yet, in some circumstances, these resources are not enough and we must reach for something more. We must access, or are forced to access, the spiritual realm. We seek our Higher Power, with an emphasis on *power.*

Accessing the spiritual realm may mean

- connecting to our ancestors, especially those who were brave in their time;
- connecting to the greater good that makes our risk necessary;
- connecting to our spiritual heroes;
- connecting to the presence of God in our time of trial;
- connecting to wisdom and moral clarity that show us the way forward; or
- connecting to our bodies to strengthen and empower us in mysterious ways.

In all these ways—and others—the spiritual realm can help us acquire the courage we need in our time of testing. Nurturing these connections prepares us for the inevitable times of trial to come.

So, how do we access the spiritual realm?

I am amazed how often people who have done courageous things say that they had a strength, or an endurance, or a vision that was beyond their ordinary abilities and resources, that enabled them to do things that amazed even them. Sometimes they say they were possessed by a power greater than themselves. "It was not me, it was Christ acting through me," as one Christian friend of mine said. Such comments give us a clue regarding the dynamics of spiritual power.

Through prayer, meditation, rites of various kinds, or other spiritual disciplines, we empty ourselves. Prayers of surrender create space within us, space for God to enter and "empower us." Only as we surrender, surrender our need for control, surrender our fear, and surrender our ego can we create the space courage will fill, space for the Divine Love to infuse us with power. It is a truism of spiritual work that sometimes we have to

surrender in order to find,
lose in order to gain,
die in order to live, and
be weak in order to be strong.

Some crises in life come upon us so fast that we have no time to do spiritual work. We are not prepared. This is all the more reason, then, to give regular attention to our spiritual needs so that when a crisis comes we will have the spiritual resources that make courage possible.

Our time of testing will come. And our Higher Power is waiting patiently to come alongside us and empower us to act courageously in love. However, whether we find the courage to act appropriately or we shrink away in fear, or even if we do a little of both, we can be sure that whatever happens, whatever actions we take, and however our choices turn out, we never walk alone. We live and die in the arms of Eternal Love.

Reflection Questions and Activities

1. In your journal, write about a time in your life when you did something risky, something you thought you could never do. What was the context? Where did you find the courage you needed?
2. Identify a context that requires a person to have courage just to live.
3. Soldiers often sing as they march off to war. Music is a great source of inspiration. What songs, hymns, folk music, or national tunes inspire you and give you courage?
4. Reflect on the phrase “the courage to be wrong.” Can you give some examples?
5. Stories about courage are frequently set in the context of war, conflict, or death. Who is your favorite movie character who was brave in one of these situations?

18

Significance

Accepting the Radical Significance of Our Lives

Human life is insignificant. We humans are especially insignificant in the context of the grand scheme of things. This is a hard realization to embrace—our ancestors blindly thought humans were the center of the universe—but it is important to come to terms with our insignificance and therefore with our need for significance.

What do I mean by the word "significant"?

- We use the term "significant other" to describe someone *important* to us.
- We say that a sequence of events was significant, meaning that it revealed a *purpose.*
- Saying something is significant can be another way of saying it is *meaningful.*

The term "significant" is used here not so much in the sense of "I am important," although that is part of the meaning, but in the sense of "*my life* is significant." Purpose is another aspect of significance. Young people often hint at this aspect when they say, "I want to make a difference." The same meaning is used when seniors pen their memoirs or write their own obituary. They wonder if the world is any better for their having passed through it. All this reflects our spiritual need for significance. We ask ourselves, Is my life significant?

Modern civilization has sharpened our need for significance. With today's communications technology and information available at our fingertips, we are keenly aware that over eight billion human beings live on this planet, give or take a few hundred thousand. This awareness sharpens the question of whether our own life is significant. Indeed, an individual life can look pretty cheap (or insignificant) when viewed on the world stage.

Science is exploring the cosmos. Thanks to the *Voyager* robot probe, Carl Sagan showed us that earth is but "a little blue dot" in the vast emptiness of the universe. Everything we hold significant—those we love and all our collective lives, past and present—has occurred on that little blue dot. We conclude that humanity is rather insignificant on the cosmic scale. All the while, we search for life, especially intelligent life, among the billions and billions of stars and millions of galaxies. Yet, so far, all our radio signals have fallen on deaf ears, if there is life with "ears" out there at all. Are we alone in the universe? Isn't the search for extraterrestrial life really a search for humanity's significance?

How many humans have lived and died on this planet Earth? A rough estimate is 110 billion. Some of those were noteworthy and have made it into the history books. Most individuals been rather insignificant historically. Most of us today will not make it into the history books either. All we can hope for is to be remembered by our loved ones for a few years, perhaps a generation. What is the significance of one person's life in the context of evolutionary time? What makes one life significant and not another?

Today, more and more of us live in large cities where we have limited, fragmented communities and pluralistic values. We are identified by our ID numbers and passwords. Millions are drawn to social media as a way to be noticed and remembered and to feel significant and unique. Advertisers tell us all the time that we are special, unique, and deserve this product or that vacation or this particular privilege. Privilege becomes a substitute for significance (if I am privileged, I must be significant). Similarly, fame is pitched to us, particularly to young people, as a path to lasting significance, such as the fame that comes from being the latest rock star, sports hero, or TV personality. Fame is a shallow substitute for a life of significance. It is a temporary fix at best, a significance that will end with the next news cycle, or the next TV season, or the next generation.

So, significance has emerged as the spiritual need of the twenty-first century. Our need for significance may be a carryover from an earlier religious age, when our ancestors believed everything that happened to them was significant, meant something. Now, we are not sure that anything is meaningful, especially our lives. We may echo the thoughts of Shakespeare's Macbeth from centuries earlier that life is all too short and a tale told by an idiot, full of meaningless words and pointless activities, signifying nothing. (Shakespear, *Macbeth*, act 5, scene 5).

Some of us are quite fortunate in that we had loving and protective parents who helped us feel special, who looked upon our existence with delight.

- Some of us have been fortunate enough to have been successful in school and/or in our career.
- A few of us have made contributions to our communities, our nation, or our institutions that will be noted in history books.
- Many more of us, who live ordinary lives, draw our sense of significance from the children we have raised or the money we have earned or the families we belong to.

Many of us did not have loving parents or experience much success in our adult lives or do not currently belong to a family that values us. For such people, the need for significance may be more acute and may, if not resolved, contribute to depression, self-destructive behavior, or even suicide. The modern age, despite all its benefits, has fostered a growing mental health crisis, or shall I say a spiritual crisis that is centered on the question, "Is my life significant?" Resolving the need to feel that our life has significance is not easily remedied by human means or human circumstances. For many of us, our significance must ultimately come from elsewhere.

One of the ways we can embrace a sense of the significance of our lives is by participating in something larger than ourselves—a noble cause, institution, or movement that does have significance. We can devote ourselves to institutions with noble purposes, such as the military, medical institutions, universities, or museums. So, too, we can be drawn to various mass movements, political parties, social justice movements, religious crusades, or environmental causes. Thousands of nonprofit organizations, large and small, national and international, appeal to our need for significance. Most of them do not pay much, but they offer employees, volunteers, and donors a chance to make a difference. As with so many other "pitches" we receive, we must be good consumers because "significance" is a neutral word. There is good significance and bad significance. The history books will remember the dictators of the world as much as the saints. We must temper our need for significance with wise ethical considerations.

Western cultures place great value upon the individual compared to earlier or more collectively oriented cultures. Such individualism, along with secularism and pluralism, has robbed Westerners of many of the sources of significance that both earlier humans around the world and contemporary non-Western humans embrace. In this way, the modern cultural emphasis on the individual has intensified the search for significance. Yet, in other ways, the Western emphasis upon the value of the individual, embedded in the Western democracies and reflected in theistic religions, is quite radical in the face of the reality of human insignificance.

The assertion that individual lives have significance, even in the face of our insignificance in the span of history and the universe, is really astonishing. In a sense, the fact that we humans are here at all, from the perspective of the universe and history, is a miracle. Suppose we are the only self-aware life form in the universe. If so, that "little blue dot" that Sagan spoke of, the Earth, is a miraculous place, a place to be cherished and protected—a place of great significance. Consider that in the context of the 8 billion people on Earth, or of the 110 billion people who came before us, each of us has a unique set of fingerprints, a unique history, and maybe therefore a unique soul. So, to truly satisfy our need for significance, we must reach beyond space and time and affirm with the spiritual sages of our species that we are, each of us, significant, not just because of whatever we might do or not do but simply because we live, love, and think. We can claim our significance based on the miracle that life is!

Religious traditions in the West often refer to the Book of Life, a mystical book in which God or the angels recorded each righteous person's life and deeds. Most twenty-first-century people do not see any evidence of angels or an eternal realm beyond the here and now, but it is an appealing idea that everything that each of us is—all of our loves, memories, accomplishments, and mistakes—are not lost when we die or when our webpage is deleted but is "remembered" by the Eternal One. As one theologian described it, "Nothing is forgotten" in the mind of God.

A spiritual perspective on significance suggests that this concept should not be defined solely, if at all, by historians. A spiritual perspective holds that a significant life is a life lived well, a life that is lived with

integrity,
compassion,
hope, and
growth.

This perspective changes the parameters of a significant life. In other words, the criteria for entry into the Book of Life are not the same as those for entry into history books.

I have known people whose lives finally and fully came into their significance in the very act of dying. I am thinking of men and women who sacrificed themselves for the lives, welfare, or safety of others. I am thinking of people who suffered greatly in life with horrible pain but nevertheless remained calm, joyful, and generous in spirit even up to the end. Their suffering or dying was their "finest hour," the time in their life that gave significance to all the other years that came before. Hopefully, you have been blessed by knowing a few of these martyrs and saints. How we die or what we leave to our heirs can make an otherwise insignificant life significant. And from a spiritual perspective, it is never too late to make our lives significant.

Rooting the significance of our lives in a spiritual perspective anchors us in a world that treats us as insignificant in the guise of fake significance. If we embrace significance as it is understood in spiritual terms, then we must realize that

what we do matters,
what we say matters,
what we believe matters,
what we choose matters, and
how we conduct ourselves matters.

Reflection Questions and Activities

1. Does the desire to "make a difference" resonate with you? In your journal, write about times in your life so far when you felt you made a difference in someone's life, in your own life, or in the world.
2. How can we feel significant without feeling self-important? What are the signs and symptoms of a lack of significance in the world?
3. Look up and reflect on Max Ehrmann's prose poem "Desiderata." How does this poem offer an answer to the question of what makes our

life significant? Is this a spiritual viewpoint? What other poems have contributed to your personal exploration of significance?

4. Do you express yourself artistically? Do you write, paint, sing, act, or design? Do you feel that your artistic expressions give your life significance? If you do not embrace any of the standard modes of artistic expression, is there something else that you have put your heart and soul into that gives your life significance or represents your life?

5. Is the stance that "my life has significance" ultimately an act of faith? Why or why not?

19

Compassion

Loving Others Even When They Are Difficult or Different

Humans are difficult. Oh, can they be difficult! Human beings can be irritating, obnoxious, and challenging. We must admit that each of us can ourselves be difficult in the eyes of some people. Dealing with difficult or different people is a universal feature of the human condition.

More often than not, the primary way we deal with difficult people is through suspicion, social isolation, and labeling, analyzing, and dehumanizing those we see as different. Such approaches can intensify social estrangement and alienation, fostering family estrangement and social and political divisions and ultimately leading to hatred and even war between "tribes." If we are to survive as a species, we must learn another way.

The spiritual perspective on how to meet this challenge is the way of compassion. Compassion is a spiritual need, a need that we humans must satisfy now more than ever. But compassion is hard:

- Most of us are able to love those who love us. It is much more difficult to be kind, much less love, those who don't love us, who dislike us or even hate us.
- Most of us are able to love our loved ones, our immediate family, our children, our spouse, our aging parent . . . most of the time. It is much more difficult to love those outside of our families—the neighbors

down the street, the poor family across town, the addicts who burglarized our place of business, the foreigners across the ocean.

- Most of us are able to love those who are clean, polite, speak English, and seem motivated. It is much more difficult to love those who are dirty, ill mannered, speak a foreign language, or seem lazy.
- Most of us are able to love those who are healthy and whole. It is much more difficult to love those who are sick, deformed, disabled, or dying.
- Most of us are able to love those who are easy to get along with. It is much more difficult to love those who are self-centered, talk incessantly, or are loud or condescending.
- Most of us are able to love those who are nice. It is much more difficult to love those who have an edge, who are hostile, resentful, and spiteful, who have a chip on their shoulder or an axe to grind.
- Most of us are able to love people who are like us. It is much more difficult to love those who are different in some way—a different race, different socioeconomic class, different religion, different sexual orientation, different political views—just *different.*
- Most of us are able to love cute puppies but not aggressive dogs.

You get the point.

What is compassion? It is our caring and empathetic response to the pain and suffering of another human (or animal). It begins when we look past the features or labels that irritate us or divide us from another person and see the unique person within. Perhaps we see the pain that is behind the obnoxious or off-putting behaviors. Once we see that pain, we recognize their pain as the same pain we too have on occasion. Our heart softens, and we then respond with compassion.

In one sense, compassion is natural; it is built into our DNA as humans. Yet in another, wider sense, compassion is hard. It is not natural for most of us to feel compassion for others, apart from our immediate family, and even then, we can be tested. So, to truly love another who is radically different from us and/or difficult for us to be around is hard work. Compassion is also countercultural, at least in Western culture, which values competition, aggression, and self-promotion over compassion.

Showing compassion is also risky. We might be rejected, embarrassed, or ridiculed by others. Showing compassion makes us vulnerable. Our compassion may not be welcomed. So, for all these reasons, there are times when it is just not humanly possible to love the other person. In such circumstances, we need to draw upon our spiritual resources.

The rare humans among us who are authentically and universally compassionate are called saints. But all of us know goodness when we see it. We admire people who are able to be compassionate day after day, such as in their profession or job. How do they do it? Compassion is hard, especially sustaining it over time. Such people can burn out, developing "compassion fatigue." I cannot imagine people doing these kinds of jobs without a strong and vibrant spiritual life. Even then, compassion is hard, even for the saints among us.

Compassion can also be hard for most of us because of our modern culture. The media bombard us with information about the pain and suffering of others. Even if we genuinely care, such stories are often overwhelming, and feeling compassion can be exhausting. Who can blame us for limiting our compassion to our immediate family or those who are in front of us right now?

Danny was a young man who was referred to me through a court's diversion program for his anger issues and drug abuse. His drug addiction was also being treated through a 12-step program. The counseling sessions with me were supposed to deal with his anger problems. Indeed, he was quite hostile. He certainly did not like counseling, and he probably did not like me particularly either. After all, he and I were quite different. Yet there we were—yoked together talking, sparring, and posturing, gradually forming a relationship. I used to say to myself that it was like pulling teeth. In time, Danny did share about his upbringing. I heard about his alcoholic father, family dysfunction, and neglect. Learning about the long family history of alcoholism, I came to understand that Danny's drug addiction was in part a manifestation of the family's genetics. It also became apparent that Danny had an undiagnosed attention deficit disorder (like his father), which made him prone to impulsive behaviors, the inability to sustain attention, and poor school performance. As I came to better understand Danny, my prior aversion to him faded away. He was less annoying, at least to me. My compassionate heart awakened. Danny had a lot of strikes against him in life, some of his own making but many others in the cards that had been dealt to him.

Showing compassion toward Danny, or to the Danny in your life, does not mean that we have to place ourselves in danger, blur our boundaries, stop being annoyed by them, or relieve them of their responsibility for their behavior in the past or going forward. Compassion is an attitude, not any one specific action. Compassion sees the other person "from the inside out." Seeing the other and being seen by another with this attitude does something else; it heals, it restores, and it transforms them and us. Compassion is an antidote for self-hate, which in Danny's case was huge, and loving oneself sets the foundation for a pattern of making more responsible choices.

Being compassionate can be difficult for some of us, not just because "others" are difficult but because of our own deficits. If we have not been a recipient of compassion, it is hard to give compassion to others. Frankly, some of us have been so psychologically and spiritually damaged that it is a real challenge for us to feel compassion, even for our loved ones and people like us. Compassion is like that—we have to receive some to give some, and we have to give some to receive some. However, in some people's lives, God intervenes, offering compassion to a baren soul.

Religious traditions have various words for compassion:

In the Hebrew Bible, one of God's features is lovingkindness.

Mercy is a trait of Allah.

The Christian Scriptures prefer the word love.

Compassion is central to the teachings of Buddhists.

Each of these religions describes the Divine Reality as essentially one of compassion, at least in part. Their scriptures state that God/the Creator/the Divine is the source of all compassion. God shows us compassion both collectively and individually. In the spiritual traditions of the world, our ability to be compassionate toward others, especially those who are difficult to love, is directly related to our openness to connecting with a compassionate God.

Organized religion has many faults, but it generally does testify to the importance of and availability of divine compassion, which in turn makes possible human compassion for and with difficult people or defective people and maybe even for ourselves as well. Without being reminded of this spiritual truth, how would we find the compassion to overcome the difficultness and differentness of human beings? Our ability to become one human family, the key to our survival, depends on our ability to experience divine compassion directly and authentically.

If religious talk bores you, just think of spirituality in terms of perspective. So, instead of offering conditional compassion or love, which means we love some people but not others, why not take a larger perspective, seeing all of humanity as part of one family? We all have the same emotions, fears, dreams, and hardships, and we all suffer the same ultimate fate. This larger perspective invites us to see the difficult or different other, whether near or far, as part of one family. This spiritual perspective is the foundation for compassion.

I wonder about the ways I am difficult to be around for others. I wonder about the ways that I need compassion. If truth be told, we all need compassion, first and foremost for ourselves. Self-compassion! We need to see

the inner child within us,
the hurt child,
the wounded child,
the child with dreams and fears.

We must be kind to ourselves, stop judging ourselves, and not expect perfection, however we define it. The more we are kind to ourselves, the kinder we can be to others. But it is also true that the more kindness we receive, the easier it is for us to be kind to ourselves and others. This is the circle of compassion.

Many of us ordinary people may need to begin not with more compassion but with surrender. As we surrender, we open up our hearts in ways that will allow divine compassion to flow through us. If we cannot be compassionate in our own right, maybe we can at least be a channel for divine compassion. It may be that letting compassion into our hearts will gradually transform us in wonderful and unexpected ways.

Further, we may come to see that God is to be found and experienced not just in the inner life of our soul but also in the messy process of caring for another human being. God just may show up in unexpected places—in the process, in the relationship, in the struggles, or in the very suffering of another.

Reflection Questions and Activities

1. Is compassion easy for you or difficult for you? What did your parents model for you about compassion? Discuss your experience of compassion in your family of origin with your therapist, spiritual director, or friend.

2. Watch the documentary *Won't You Be My Neighbor?* (2018) and explore the life, philosophy, and work of Fred Rogers, particularly his views on compassion and children.
3. Interview a person who must show compassion in their occupation, such as a nurse, aid worker, therapist, hospice worker, doctor, or social worker. How do they do it? How do they renew themselves? What spiritual resources do they draw upon so they are able to show compassion consistently in difficult situations or with difficult people?
4. Read the poem "Kindness" by Naomi Shihab Nye. Where does kindness or compassion come from?
5. Are there people or situations where compassion does not apply? Is compassion especially hard for men to express?

20

Roots

Cultivating a Deep and Nourishing Inner Life

HUMAN EXISTENCE IS CHARACTERIZED by change, stress, and turmoil. Sometimes the change is slow and is called growth or aging. Sometimes the change is sudden and overwhelming and is called turmoil, stress, or even trauma.

Change, stress, and turmoil are not new to humanity. They have been features of human existence since the dawn of time. To our credit, we humans have learned to adapt to change, cope with stress, and manage turmoil, enabling us to learn, grow, and build civilizations. Yet in the modern era the number of changes, the rapidity of those changes, and their foundational nature have made change more stressful. The pace of modern life, particularly in larger metropolitan areas, is fast, chaotic, and intense. The impact on us is multifold, but it particularly affects our mental and emotional well-being. Stress is a contributor to many of our modern ailments, from drug addiction to hyperactivity to heart disease.

So, because we are dealing with stress on so many levels, we humans need stability now more than ever. Yet many of the very institutions that used to provide a sense of stability or identity or continuity have themselves become unstable or are changing. We need to go deep. We need to root ourselves in the spiritual reality and the spiritual truth, in the direct, authentic, and regular experience of the Loving Presence. This love, amid the turmoil of the times, can ground us,

stabilize us,

nourish us, and

give us perspective.

I have chosen to use the metaphor of *roots* to describe this need, but I could have chosen soul, core, or identity. Roots provide stability for a tree amid the turmoil above the ground. Without roots, trees will collapse, blown over by the wind, rain, and snow. Roots go deep into the earth to provide stability. Roots also bring life-giving water to the tree through its trunk and out to its branches, allowing the tree to leaf out, grow, and reproduce itself. The deeper the roots, the more likely it is the roots will find sources of water. Roots also access nutrients in the soil, both in the organic material and even in minerals found in rocks. These resources are the chemical building blocks for the trees we see above the ground. We know now that the roots of many species of trees communicate chemically with the roots of neighboring trees of the same species. Similarly, in the realm of spirituality, all of us humans are connected or can be connected if we have deep roots.

The popular television program called *Finding Your Roots* uses modern research methods to help people identify their ancestors, giving the participants a sense of history, continuity, identity, and connection to the past. It is hard for modern, urban people to experience a sense of roots. Maybe the experience of "home" comes closest as it is the place where we say that we have roots. Home is hard to find and maintain in today's changing environment. Many of us are homeless in this sense. Yet we still need a home, a home base. So, we instinctively make a home wherever we are. A home is a place, a location, or a person that helps us

de-stress,

connect with our ancestors, and

remember who we are.

With "home" becoming more changeable, connections to our extended family less secure, and stress undermining our sense of identity and continuity, we moderns need to be intentional about developing a deep inner life. We need to grow our roots deeper and stronger into the spiritual reality and ground our sense of home, identity, stability, and peace there, not in the chaos above the ground. If we don't, we can't live, much less thrive, in the face of the levels of change and stress we live with today. Our well-being, maybe even our survival as a species, depends on going deeper.

Growing deeper roots can provide us with several benefits:

- Growing deeper roots that are grounded in the spiritual reality helps us remember who we are spiritually and celebrates a definition of ourselves that is more eternal than the multiple versions of the self that constrict and define us above the ground.
- Growing deeper roots, and visiting those roots regularly, helps us experience more stability and continuity amid the rapid and sometimes terrifying changes above the ground.
- Visiting our deeper roots helps us find silence. The aboveground world is noisy, full of disinformation, misinformation, and propaganda. We need to have periods of silence when we can clear our busy minds, gain perspective, and discern the truth—our own truth.
- Visiting our deeper roots helps us cultivate peace. The world above the ground is full of conflict and stress—in our families, in our work relationships, within ourselves, and in most institutions. The media reminds us constantly of the violence down the street and the wars around the world. We need to be able to step away and go to a peaceful place.
- Visiting our deeper roots in silence and peace creates space in which we can listen, first and foremost, to the wisdom of our body, to its pains, tensions, and sounds. Above the ground, we are too busy to listen—to our peril. Here, too, we can listen to our dreams and learn what our soul and the divine dreamer within wants to tell us. Here, in silence and peace, we can listen to the still, small voice of God within us as we slow down and take the time to pay attention.
- Cultivating our deep spiritual roots helps us heal. Slowing down the pace of life helps. Positive, peaceful thoughts help. Trusting in the goodness of the Holy One helps. Meditation practices can be a particularly helpful tool for persons struggling to be free or stay free from their cravings, obsessions, and compulsions. Addictions thrive on reactivity, as does the modern world above the ground. So, slowing down, going deep, and letting go of control help us to stop reacting and, instead, respond.

- Growing deep roots is especially helpful in our senior years as we gradually give up various identities of ourselves, even our sense of our bodily self and health. As a tree grows old, it decays and becomes more vulnerable to fire and drought. Its roots and their depth become more important. So it is with us. Deep roots can sustain us, nurturing us even as our bodies reflect the passage of time. Intriguingly, in some species of trees, like redwoods, the roots themselves become the source of new sprouts.

The great wisdom of many spiritual traditions around the world is that we can enrich, stabilize, and deepen our lives and receive the benefits noted above through regular spiritual practices aimed at the development of our deeper roots. Our roots nourish a rich inner life.

Like all the spiritual needs described in this book, our need for roots can also be misunderstood or distorted or can make us vulnerable to people with bad intentions. Our need for deeper roots may be so strong that we find conservative philosophies, reactionary leaders, and "old-time religion" very appealing. We can easily follow leaders that promise stability through returning to a more stable and secure time. Often these prophets are in religious clothing or use religious language because organized religion is a stabilizing and conservative force in most societies. We may long for the religion of our childhood, a time when life was simpler and more secure and offered the promise that things would be the same yesterday, today, and tomorrow. We find comfort in the familiar, in the hymns, norms, litanies, and established seasons of the year. As appealing as these may be, they can also be an escape from the realities of the modern world.

In contrast, a healthy spirituality rooted in our inner life, rooted in our direct experience of Divine Goodness at the ground of our being, is able to go with us into the world above the ground and become our still point in the whirlwind of modern life. This is an oscillating dynamic; go deep to renew yourself, ground yourself, and know yourself and then re-engage the world with a clear mind and loving heart. Like much of life—work and rest, sorrow and joy, independence and dependence—a healthy spirituality has a rhythm.

Change is not a bad thing. Change is life. There is no life without change. The danger is groundless, thoughtless, reactive change. Change that is gradual, thoughtful, and consensual is made possible by our deep roots in a healthy spirituality. Or, to switch to new metaphors for a minute, our inner life serves as our *anchor* in the storm of life and also as our *compass* for navigating the storm.

So, how do we develop a rich inner life? How do we grow our roots deeper into the spiritual soil? Ways we can do this include

- making regular times for meditation, prayer, and rest
- having periods of silence, times to *be*, not to *do* anything
- keeping a journal, particularly a gratitude journal
- seeing a therapist, especially an analytical therapist
- working with an interfaith spiritual director or guide
- identifying and practicing various forms of prayer (find one that fits you)
- enjoying the arts, live music, drama, and literature
- developing an artistic outlet for yourself
- spending time in nature
- reading for pleasure
- turning off the TV one night a week
- nurturing your body
- keeping the Sabbath

When I was a child and was acting out of control, my mother used to give me a "time-out." I experienced it as punishment, but my mother wanted me to learn to calm myself down. This is a useful, very important skill, one I wish I had learned better. Some people find that their prayers are done in haste. They rush through their petitions and requests, never pausing long enough to just *be* in prayer. Others don't develop a rich inner life until they hit bottom. May you not wait so long to learn this lesson. Indeed, may all of us start now, if we haven't already, to fulfill our spiritual need for deep roots in consistent, healthy, and life-affirming ways.

Reflection Questions and Activities

1. How do you cope with the stresses and changes of modern life? What practices have you found helpful?

2. Reflect on this statement: divine reality is found not just in Father Sky but also in Mother Earth.
3. Identify someone in your life who is incredibly peaceful. Interview that person. Try to understand what they do to maintain their peaceful orientation to life.
4. Choose one or two of the suggestions in this chapter for developing deeper roots and do it for twenty-one days. Log your results and your inner feelings.
5. If your life is very busy, an easy way to learn centering, relaxing, and meditation skills is to listen to one of the many podcasts on this topic available in an app store. Download one or several. Create some space and listen. Let the app be your guide.

21

Perspective

Opening to a Spirituality Suitable for the Times

We humans are myopic. We have a chronic case of tunnel vision; we focus only on what is in front of us in the moment, our personal, immediate needs. In short, we are myopic by nature and fail to see the big picture. This is part of the human condition.

In our exploration of the previous twenty spiritual needs, we have encountered the word "perspective" many times. We have seen how gaining a larger or different perspective is interwoven with satisfying various spiritual needs. I want to focus in this chapter on perspective as a spiritual need in and of itself and also describe four features of a spirituality that is healthy and life-affirming, one suitable for the challenges of the twenty-first century. But let's start with perspective as a spiritual need, using the example of a young woman I will call Jordan.

At sixteen years old, Jordan's whole life was high school, the girls' volleyball team, cheer squad, classes, and her various friends. She did not realize how limited and narrow her world was until years later, after she had attended college for a while, studied history, made friends with people from various cultural and racial backgrounds, traveled a bit, and tried and failed in several jobs and love relationships. As it turns out, life is not as simple as it was for her in high school. "Adult life is a lot more complicated," she noted. When she went to her ten-year high school reunion, she found the world of high school to be small, narrow, and self-absorbed. Symbolically, she noted how physically small the school's hallways and classrooms seemed now in comparison to how they had seemed when she was a student there. Most of us can identify with this experience. It is a natural part of growing up into adulthood (and having an adult brain). As we get older, we do tend to gain wider perspectives on many things—including the size of the hallways at our alma mater.

Jordan gained perspective naturally by getting an education, by studying history, by encountering other cultures, by meeting people who saw the world differently than her, and by reflecting critically upon herself. Many people do not have the advantage of these processes or do not benefit from them. Their perspective on life remains parochial. They tend to see things from the perspective or vantage point of a limited worldview and are thus subject to the biases, assumptions, and distortions of that worldview.

We humans have the capacity to embrace larger perspectives. We have the ability to act on the basis of the needs of the many instead of the needs of the few (or the one). We sometimes go to war based on our embracing a national perspective, seeking what is best for the nation. Successful sports teams encourage their players to embrace the perspective of the team—to work as a team and put aside their individual glory, stats, or salary negotiations. When we act on the basis of such larger perspectives, our actions are often considered noble. We may even be honored and celebrated as the best of humanity, even when the larger cause is largely one-sided.

While there are many natural forces in human life that help us gain perspective and overcome our myopia, the challenges of the twenty-first century demand from us an even broader, wider perspective—a spiritual perspective. This spiritual perspective, if it is to be healthy and life-affirming, needs to be characterized by four features.

First, a healthy, life-affirming spirituality is a *spiritual perspective*. From this perspective, we see the sacred in the material world. In a world that rushes toward, celebrates, and obsesses over all things material, we who are spiritual must have a spiritual perspective that allows us to see beyond the material to a deeper reality. Yes, we see the material world, but we also see beyond the material world to

- beauty, which is everywhere—if we can see it,
- wonder, which is everywhere—if we take the time to look, and
- mystery, which is everywhere—if our eyes (and minds) are open.

Every moment, every task, however mundane, and every relationship, however troubled, is sacred as well as material, extraordinary as well as ordinary, and full of lessons as well as failures and the holy as well as the profane. Yes, modern life can be ugly, cruel, and chaotic, but a spiritual perspective helps us see the presence, influence, and work of God, even in these negative times and invites us to join God in God's work in the world.

With a spiritual perspective, we can see our fellow human beings with "a third eye," seeing beyond their corporal existence, beyond their appearance or accomplishments, to their inner life, their spirit, where God is present and at work in their lives. Seeing others as spiritual beings means seeing them as precious, unique, eternal. Human lives have great value! Each person has dignity and worth. We must work against the dehumanizing tendencies of the modern world, which

classify us by our differences,
label us winners or losers,
treat us only as consumers, and
demand uniformity and conformity.

Similarly, we can also see ourselves as spiritual beings, connected to the Divine Love, created with intention and worth. We thus can accept our mistakes and rejoice in the lessons learned, with our journey enriched and our character strengthened. We can reject perfectionism in any form. We can understand that a life well lived is a life lived with honor, goodness, integrity, and creative expression.

Second, a spirituality relevant to these times must have a *global perspective*. It must help us to see that we all live on one small, fragile planet with limited resources. We can see that we are all interconnected because we are all affected by

- the homelessness in a nearby city,
- the famine in a far-off country,
- the polluting of the oceans, and
- the lack of a public health infrastructure.

The lack of economic justice and equality anywhere impacts all of us. There is no escaping it. Isolation is not possible. We need to realize that we all live in one community. It is not enough to have a national perspective, however noble that might be; we must now shift to a global perspective. Instead of America first, a spiritual perspective embraces Earth first.

Third, we must have a *temporal perspective* that helps us put the present moment into the broad context of time. The modern culture of the twenty-first-century, despite its wealth of knowledge, tends to reinforce a focus on the present, on the urgency of the present moment. This urgency shapes us to want

the quick fix,
the instant solution,
easy credit, and
fast food.

When we rush in to fix problems quickly, we often fail to understand the history of the problem, the complexities, the various possible solutions, and the value of a long-term solution. In other words, we have a narrow perspective. Quick, uninformed action often leads to unintended consequences.

Consumed with the present, we forget all the lessons of the past, both our personal history and our collective history. When we ignore, forget, or do not correctly understand these lessons, we are prone to repeat the same mistakes over and over again. History does have lessons to teach us, but not many of us are students of history, either of our collective history or of our personal histories.

A temporal perspective also helps us think carefully and soberly about the future. People who work with trees like to say that "the best time to plant a tree is twenty years ago" because it takes time for a tree to mature enough to provide its full benefits of shade, carbon reduction, biodiversity, etc. Tree people tend to have a temporal perspective. They are always thinking ahead fifty years.

Making decisions with this kind of long-term perspective requires that we have patience, that we put aside our expectations for immediate results, invest for the long term, and build habits of living that will sustain our health into the future. We need to appreciate the process, the value of small, consistent change, and not be narrowly focused on the end results. From a spiritual perspective, the process is equally important to the goal.

Seniors are often more interested in history than their younger selves were. Our elders often have the perspective of the years they have lived. With the perspective of time comes the virtue of wisdom. My mother, amid the sorrows and health challenges of her later years, repeatedly said, "This too shall pass." This may sound like a cliché, but it was also true on several levels. Certainly, my mother had lived enough years to have a larger perspective on life's difficulties. But a temporal perspective such as she had can also help us realize that even the good times do not last forever. With this realization, we are prompted to make the most of the good times—

the tender moments,

the special memories, and

the times of closeness.

Parents know this truth. When their children are young, as the saying goes, "The days are long, but the years are short."

Finally, a life-affirming spirituality also has a *cosmic perspective*. A cosmic perspective helps us see our lives in the context of the universe, embracing how insignificant but precious our lives are. A cosmic perspective helps us see that we are part of the biosphere of this planet. We are part of its life and are connected through the tree of life with all other creatures great and small. We understand that life is a gift, that life is sacred, and we embrace a reverence for life in its many forms. Our spirituality encourages us to be good stewards of the Earth and all its living things.

A wise woman once told me, when I was in the midst of a life crisis, to calm down, pause, and see things from God's perspective. God's perspective is *spiritual, global, temporal,* and *cosmic*. These four characteristics distinguish a life-affirming spirituality from a toxic one. We should reject any spirituality or religion or prophet that does not embrace these four features. Be a wise consumer!

It is interesting how many religious traditions around the globe use the metaphors of light, of enlightenment, or of seeing to explain their convictions and practices. In many traditions, spiritual guides are called seers or visionaries. In some ways, at its core, spirituality is about seeing the world and ourselves from a larger and yet deeper perspective. Once we have this enlightenment, we cannot go back to the narrow, materialistic, urgent perspective. Once we see the true size of the halls at our former high school, we cannot go back to our innate myopia.

Reflection Questions and Activities

1. Describe a time when you realized that your previous perspective was narrow and limiting. How did you come to this larger perspective?

2. The 1946 black-and-white film *It's a Wonderful Life* is filled with spiritual truths (but also some blind spots) that have made it an enduring classic at the holidays. It illustrates several of the spiritual needs described in this book. In what way is the film primarily about perspective, and how does it show that when we gain a new spiritual perspective, many other lessons flow?
3. Are you interested in learning a language other than your native tongue? The best way to learn it is through cultural immersion. In that way, you not only master a tool but also learn how people in another culture think, see their world, and structure their reality.
4. How have you honored your past, your pains and joys and your successes and lessons learned? What lessons have you learned from your personal history? Make a list of your life lessons.
5. Read a book or view a documentary on cosmology, the nature of the universe, as it is presently understood. Carl Sagan's *Cosmos* is an easy-to-read book, or you could watch the TV series. How does this perspective inform your spirituality?

22

Beauty

Turning to Beauty as a Spiritual Tool

LIFE IS FULL OF beauty. Life can be ugly, but human existence is filled with incredible beauty—a sunset, a baby's smile, great music, delicate butterflies. We humans are programmed to notice beauty. Our eyes respond to varieties of color, texture, and shape, and our ears notice the nuances of sound. We are drawn to beauty naturally. In the presence of beauty,

we stop,
    we pause, and
        we smile.

Our stress lessens. We may even connect briefly with another time and place.

Our ancestors' first experience of beauty was in the natural world. Beauty appeared to them in the views of sunsets, starry nights, and flowers, in the songs of birds and the wind, and in the patterns of birds in flight, fires, sand dunes, and rhythmic waves on shorelines. These are all beautiful in their own right, and they are the raw material from which we humans create beauty ourselves, such as music, the visual arts, and the written arts in the forms of poetry, literature, and drama.

What exactly is beauty? It is partly *order*—patterns formed and arranged in a symmetry that is pleasing to the eye, ear, or mind. Beauty is also about the complexity and nuances of the perceptual data we receive from our *senses,* especially color, sound, touch, and sight. Beauty is also partly *delight*, something that is desirable and pleasing.

Why do we humans have an innate capacity for recognizing beauty, even seeing beauty when it is not evident upon a detailed analysis? Might not our appreciation of beauty be another footprint of the Creator upon our souls? That footprint has fashioned within us a spiritual need for beauty.

We humans do not always make or keep things beautiful. In fact, we are pretty messy creatures! Yet it is also true that beauty is calming and healing. Beauty decreases anxiety, stress, and depression. Beautiful environments uplift our spirits and make us behave better so that we act civilized and are more respectful toward one another and nature. Beauty brings out the best in us. Consider beauty, if you will, a part of our spiritual nature, our higher selves.

Moreover, beauty invites participation. We listen to stories, read poems, sing songs, study paintings, decorate our bodies, and even dance together. The more we participate in beauty, the more healing and restorative beauty becomes. *Beauty invites beauty!* Moreover, beauty invites us to make beauty, to create beauty, to be artistic. The opportunity to create beauty, to make art, is also therapeutic, healing, and restorative, similar to observing beauty. Being creative allows us to express ourselves at the deepest levels and reveal inner truths about our soul not otherwise acknowledged by our conscious mind. The school of psychotherapy called art therapy uses music therapy and writing or storytelling as therapy. Creating beauty, creating art, is therapeutic.

It's sad, isn't it, that the people who need this kind of healing the most—prisoners, the elderly, the sick and dying, victims of violence and war, and the poor—often live in institutional environments devoid of beauty and/or have few opportunities for creative expression. And yet at the same time, some of the most inspiring art has been created by people trapped in such circumstances, which testifies to the enduring strength of the human spirit.

Beauty, art, and spirituality are interwoven in all cultures and religions and in all of history. The mystical experience of the Holy often compels us to create something tangible to mark the encounter, to be a visible symbol of the invisible reality. In turn, great religious art seeks to recreate a spiritual experience for subsequent generations,

each time they listen to the music,
visit the monument, or
tell the sacred story again.

Beauty is a pathway to God, a glimpse of the Divine.

Of course, not all art is religious, but all art can be spiritual. Great art is often described as timeless. It connects us to truths, insights, and a spiritual perspective on the human condition. Art is the bridge between the *material world* and the *spiritual world*. The spiritual world is not easily experienced directly nor easily described in everyday language. The world of the sacred is the world of mystery, symbol, and subtlety. Such truths are better communicated through the arts than through historical or scientific language.

Art serves as a bridge in part because it employs nonlinear, indirect, symbolic, and even nonverbal language. Art is the language of spiritual conversation. For example, the art of poetry employs the language of metaphor, symbol, allegory, and paradox. Science and philosophy say, "God is . . . ," whereas the poet says, "God is like . . ." Spirituality is mysterious. God is ultimately a mystery, as is life and death and new birth and redemption. The arts give us a way to talk about or represent these mysteries, the otherwise unknowable.

If art is the bridge between the material and spiritual worlds, the traffic on this bridge goes in both directions. *Receiving beauty* and *creating beauty* are the two directions we can travel over this bridge. At a basic level, then, art or beauty is more than a spiritual need, although it is that. It is also a form of communication, a tool for exploring all the spiritual needs described in this book. *The arts are the language of spirituality*. We use the arts to describe our spiritual experiences:

to tell stories about the *meaning* (chapter 1) of unexpected events,

to play music to give us *courage* (chapter 17),

to engage in ritual dance to express our *oneness* (chapter 11),

to create paintings to capture wonder (chapter 7), and

to design buildings or monuments to be timeless or *transcendent* (chapter 4).

When we *receive* art, when we enter into the art, we open ourselves up to the experience or soul of the artist and the interpreters of that art—the actors, the readers, the musicians, and the dancers. We take in what the art is communicating about life, the human condition, and that which is eternal. The best art, the most lasting creative works, are those that not only re-create the emotional-spiritual experience of the artist but also touch something eternal. This is especially true when the art is religious, when the artist is expressing their experience of the Divine.

When we *create* art, we are similarly expressing the deepest and even the mysterious parts of ourselves, our soul, and are articulating that message in the form of our chosen artistic medium. Musicians and actors create art. We too can create art in hundreds of small and large ways. The process of creating is itself, for many, a spiritual experience because it forces us to go deep, to touch on themes that are true not only for us but for others as well, as if we are offering to the world what is sacred to us. Our artistic creations reflect our soul.

It is true that tastes in art change over the generations. Later generations may not connect as easily to a particular work of art as their grandparents did. On the other hand, some works of art that were initially not conceived of as religious or spiritual may be experienced that way by future generations. Art as a language of spirituality is like that. Links are forged in both directions. Art is a process. Art is open-ended, always subject to new interpretations and meanings. Art is a process because art is primary communication, the language of spirituality.

Not everyone is artistic, or appreciates art, or thinks art is an important part of a society. Yet people are often more artistic or creative than they think they are. It is just a matter of tapping into your soul and finding a comfortable medium to express yourself in.

I first met Billy when he came to my home to service our furnace. We got to talking, and he learned that I was a therapist. Three weeks later, he asked to see me professionally, sharing that he had had a vision (a dream) three times in the last few months that was frightening him.

Billy was a thirty-four-year-old single man with a high school education. His younger sister had died of drug overdose, and his parents were elderly and lived out of state. He seemed mildly depressed and, as he said, a bit frightened. His vision was of a foggy mountain meadow, in which he was barely able to make out the shapes of trees and the surroundings. He reported that it was a very vivid vision in pastel colors, with no plot or sounds . . . just a bright vision. His sense was that something was about to come to him through the fog, something frightening.

After exploring Billy's vision, his life, and current stressors, I suggested that if the vision came to him again, he should try to stay with it and let it unfold further. The next time we met, Billy came to the session with a large roll of art paper. He had created a watercolor painting of his vision. I was surprised and delighted that he had so boldly decided to face his fears in this way. He apologized for his poor painting skill, saying he had never done anything like it before, so the painting was only a reasonable facsimile. We explored the painting in front of us. We noted that there was clearly light behind the fog, as if it was morning and the sun had just risen and was shining through the morning mist. This interpretation helped dissipate his fear, but he still felt that the meaning of the vision was that something important was coming out of the fog to him. We explored various people or things that might be coming to him.

The next time I saw Billy, he brought with him the same large painting, but now he also brought his watercolor paint set. Laying it out on the coffee table between us, I invited him to continue his painting. He did so, painting in the same impressionistic style, but as he added layers to it, the image evolved. Some figures began to emerge, figures he called angels. We explored that theme the rest of our time: what message might these angels be bringing to him?

In sequent sessions, he continued the process of adding to the painting off and on throughout our conversation. As he added additional layers, other figures became clear, first of his mother, then his deceased sister, and then some animals. These revelations led to some very fruitful and powerful conversations about and with his loved ones. He did good work therapeutically. It was really fascinating to see the painting take on a life of its own. Week after week, it became the tool or platform upon which Billy did his soul work.

I did not see Billy again for several months. When I next saw him, he was dating a woman and seemed much happier. He had kept his multilayered watercolor and had even made a crude frame for it. We never quite figured out who or what was coming to him that had prompted such a powerful vision many months earlier. My final interpretation is that whoever or whatever was coming to him through the fog was secondary to the primary message of hope. The point of the vision was for him to initiate the process of recapturing a sense of hope in his life, the belief that something good was just around the corner.

So, beauty is a need, but more than that, it is a tool, a tool we can use to access and enhance all of the spiritual needs described in this book. It is also a bridge between the spiritual world and the material world. May you travel across this bridge regularly.

Reflection Questions and Activities

1. How do you express your creativity? Do you have hobbies? Have you ever felt "inspired" in the process of creating? What was that like?
2. Reflect on this phrase: beauty is to the soul as food is to the body.
3. I've mentioned works of art, mostly movies, plays, or poems, in many of the "Reflection Questions and Activities" at the end of each chapter in this book. Looking back, which works of art seem to enrich the spiritual need of a particular chapter the most for you? Which ones touched you in some unexpected way? You may also wish to explore the lists of films and poems in the bibliography.
4. What is the connection between artistic creativity and adversity? Do you think adversity suppresses creativity or sparks it? How?
5. If you are not artistic, here is a simple way to start. Keep a journal and write in it every day, telling the journal about your day, your year, your life. Keep it private. Or, if you prefer structure, start each entry with one of the needs described in the twenty-two chapters in this book. Let your soul speak.

More Resources

Movies

Movies are powerful artistic tools since they can blend great storytelling, acting, the visual arts, and music. Further, the more memorable movies often explore one or more spiritual needs. Here are some films I have found formative in my spiritual journey. I have classified them by their primary spiritual focus.

Meaning

Forrest Gump (1994)

Wisdom

Passengers (2008)

Transcendence

Mr. Holland's Opus (1995)

Purpose

Simon Birch (1998)

Hope

West Side Story (1961, 2021), *Dr. Zhivago* (1965)

Wonder

Jurassic Park (1993), *Interstellar* (2014)

Explanations

The Truman Show (1998), *The Matrix* (1999), *What the Bleep Do We Know?* (2004)

Courage

Schindler's List (1993), *Lincoln* (2012)

Compassion

E.T. the Extra-Terrestrial (1982), *The Green Mile* (1999), *Up* (2009), *Inside Out* (2015)

Transformation

Shawshank Redemption (1994), *Good Will Hunting* (1997)

Connections

Field of Dreams (1989), *Ghost* (1990)

Forgiveness

Ordinary People (1980), *Terms of Endearment* (1983), *The Mission* (1986), *The Power of Forgiveness* (documentary, 2008)

Gratitude

Amelie (2001), *The Bucket List* (2007), *Soul* (2020)

Peace

Eat, Pray Love (2010)

Oneness

Grapes of Wrath (1940), *Remember the Titans* (2000), *Everything Everywhere All at Once* (2022)

Deliverance

Deliverance (1972), *Clean and Sober* (1988), *The Pursuit of Happyness* (2006)

Perspective

It's a Wonderful Life (1946), *The Arrival* (1996), *Life Is Beautiful* (1997)

Poetry

Poems are an artistic tool that we can use to explore our spiritual needs. Here are some poems I have found to be spiritually enlightening. Some are mentioned earlier in this book. Most of these poems are available online.

Camus, Albert. “Invincible Summer.”

Ehrmann, Max. “Desiderata.”

Eliot, T. S. “We Shall Not Cease” from *Litle Gidding*.

Gibran, Khalil. “Fear.”

Gibson, Andrea. “Love Letter from the Afterlife.”

Hafiz. “All the Hemispheres.”

Keithley, Zanna. “Overcoming Fear.”

Levetov, Denise. “The Avowal.”

———. “Primary Wonder.”

Milosz, Czeslaw. “Awakening.”

Nye, Naomi Shihab. “Kindness.”

Oliver, Mary. “Mysterious, Yes.”

———. “When I Am among the Trees.”

———. “Wild Geese.”

Puorro, Gina. “A Playful Love Poem to Death.”

Richardson, Jan. “How the Light Comes.”

Sexton, Anne. “Welcome Morning.”

Stafford, William. “The Way It Is.”

Wahtola Trommer, Rosemerry. “Consecration.”

Music

Below is a list of 22 popular songs, one per artist, in the last 80 years or so. Some you may be familiar with; others not so much. As you listen to them, reflect on which spiritual need or needs they speak to or help you explore. Most of these songs are available on the internet.

Animals. “House of the Rising Sun.”

Louis Armstrong. “What a Wonderful World.”

Joan Baez. “All my Trials.”

Beatles. “Let it be.”

David Bowe. "Heroes."

Eric Clapton. "Tears in Heaven."

Kelly Clarkson. "Meaning of Life."

Leonard Cohen. "Hallelujah."

Bob Dylan. "Blowin' in the Wind."

Eminem. "Not Afraid."

Fleetwood Mac. "Landside."

Michael Jackson. "Man in the Mirror."

John Lennon. "Imagine."

Bob Marley. "One Love."

Bette Milder. "Wind Beneath my Wings."

Joni Mitchell. "I Think I Understand."

Johnny Nash. "I Can See Clearly Now."

Linkin Park. "In the End."

Rolling Stones. "Satisfaction."

Simon and Garfunkel. "Bridge over Troubled Waters."

Bruce Springsteen. "The River."

Taylor Swift. "Change."

Bibliography

Allport, Gordon W. *The Individual and His Religion: A Psychological Interpretation*. New York: Macmillan, 1967.

Beattie, Melody. *The Language of Letting Go: Daily Meditations on Codependency*. New York: Spiegel & Grau, 2025.

Becker, Ernest. *The Denial of Death*. New York: Free Press. 1997.

Bianchi, Eugene C. *Aging as a Spiritual Journey*. Eugene, OR: Wipf & Stock, 2011.

Borg, Marcus J. *Days of Awe and Wonder: How to be a Christian in the 21st Century*. New York: HarperCollins. 2017.

Buettner, Dan. *The Blue Zones Secrets for Living Longer: Lessons from the Healthiest Places on Earth*. Washington, DC: National Geographic. 2023.

Cobb, John B., Jr., and David Ray Griffin. *Process Theology: An Introductory Exposition*. Philadelphia: Westminster Press, 1976.

Dalai Lama [Tenzin Gyatso] and Desmond Tutu. *The Book of Joy: Lasting Happiness in a Changing World*. New York: Avery, 2016.

Emmons, Robert A. *Thanks! How the New Science of Gratitude Can Make You Happier*. Boston: Houghton Mifflin, 2007.

Fitchett, George. *Assessing Spiritual Needs: A Guide for Caregivers*. Lima, OH: Academic Renewal Press, 2002.

Fowler, Jame W. *Stages of Faith: The Psychology of Human Development and the Quest for Meaning*. New York: HarperCollins, 1995.

Gibran, Kahlil. *The Prophet*. New York: Alfred A. Knopf, 1923.

Hanh, Thich Nhat. *Living Buddha, Living Christ*. New York: Riverhead Books, 1995.

Hirsh, Sandra Krebs, and Jane A. G. Kise. *Soul Types: Matching Your Personality and Spiritual Path*. Minneapolis: Augsburg Books, 2006.

Jones, Russell Siler. *Spirit in Session: Working with Your Client's Spirituality (and Your Own) in Psychotherapy*. West Conshohocken, PA: Templeton Press, 2019.

Keen, Sam. *Apology for Wonder*. New York: Harper & Row. 1969.

Liebert, Eilzabeth. *Changing Life Patterns: Adult Development in Spiritual Direction*. St. Louis: Chalice Press, 2006.

Luskin, Fred. *Forgive for Good: A Proven Prescription for Health and Happiness*. New York: HarperCollins, 2002.

Manning, Brennan. *The Ragamuffin Gospel*. Colorado Springs, CO: Multnomah Books, 2005.

Merton, Thomas. *A Year with Thomas Merton: Daily Meditations from His Journals*. Edited by Jonathan Montaldo. San Francisco: HarperSanFrancisco, 2004.

Mitchell, Kenneth R., and Herbert Anderson. *All Our Losses, All Our Griefs: Resources for Pastoral Care*. Louisville, KY: Westminster John Knox Press, 1983.

Moore, Thomas. *Care of the Soul: A Guide for Cultivating Depth and Sacredness in Everyday Life*. New York: HarperCollins, 1992.

Peck, M. Scott. *The Road Less Traveled: A New Psychology of Love, Traditional Values, and Spiritual Growth*. New York: Touchstone, 2003.

Rohr, Richard. *Breathing Under Water: Spirituality and the Twelve Steps*. Cincinnati: Franciscan Media, 2011.

Sullender, R. Scott. *Ancient Sins . . . Modern Addictions: A Fresh Look at the Seven Deadly Sins*. Eugene, OR: Cascade Books, 2013.

———. *Losses in Later Life: A New Way of Walking with God*. 2nd edition. Eugene, OR: Wipf and Stock. 2020.

———. *Trauma and Grief: Resources and Strategies for Ministry*. Eugene, OR: Cascade Books, 2018.

Thurman, Howard. *Jesus and the Disinherited*. Boston: Beacon Press, 1996.

Tillich, Paul. *The Courage to Be*. New Haven, CT: Yale University Press, 2014.

Tyson, Neil deGrasse. *Starry Messenger: Cosmic Perspectives on Civilization*. New York: Henry Holt & Co., 2022.

Zinn, Jon Kabat. *Wherever You Go, There You Are: Mindfulness Meditation in Everyday Life*. New York: Hachette Books, 2014.

www.ingramcontent.com/pod-product-compliance
Lightning Source LLC
LaVergne TN
LVHW012331100826
845148LV00017B/2111

* 9 7 9 8 3 8 5 2 6 6 9 1 3 *